Surviving the Unthinkable

Surviving the Unthinkable

The Loss of a Child

A Gentle, Practical Guide for Mothers, Family, and Friends

Janice Bell Meisenhelder

Library of Congress Control Number: 2016914028
MBM Publishers, Wellesley, Massachusetts
Meisenhelder, Janice Bell, author
Surviving the Unthinkable: The Loss of a Child / Janice Bell Meisenhelder

IBSN-13: 9780979651120
ISBN-10: 0979651123

Contents

Preface ix

Part 1: A Survival Guide for Mothers 1
  Chapter 1:   The Unimaginable .3
    Initial Shock 3
    Rhythms of Grief 5
    The Pain of Loss 6
    Common Physical Reactions 10
    Common Cognitive Reactions 13
    Hunger and Yearning for Your Child 15
    How Do I Go On? 18
  Chapter 2:   Anger, Guilt, Envy, and Anxiety 21
    Anger 21
    Guilt 24
    Envy 27
    Anxiety 29
  Chapter 3:   Triggers and Holidays 32
    Triggers 32
    The Grave 34
    Your Child's Belongings .36
    Holidays and Family Events 38
    Your Child's Birthday 43

Chapter 4:   Loss: A Spiritual Crisis 48
    How Can This Happen?. 48
    How Could God Allow This? 49
    The Faith Factor 50
    Where Is My Child Now? 51
    Spiritual Signs and Messages. 52
    Finding Hope 55
Chapter 5:   Dodging Negative Messages 58
    The "Closure" Myth. 58
    Judgmental Religion 59
    Denying the Intensity of Loss 60
    Faith Healing. 62
Chapter 6:   Hurtful Responses. 64
    Fix-It Friends. 64
    Clueless Family Members 66
    Needy Grievers 67
    The Timid and Frightened 69
    The Judges. 70
Chapter 7:   Your Identity 72
    Who Am I Now?. 72
    Impact on Self-Esteem. 73
Chapter 8:   Helping Your Children and Spouse. 76
    Your Surviving Children 76
    Husbands and Partners 80
    Single Moms 87
Chapter 9:   Honoring Your Child 90
Chapter 10: Coping over Time: Changes in Grief. 94
Chapter 11: The First Anniversary 98
Chapter 12: Second-Year Losses 103

Unrealistic Expectations 103
Secondary Losses. 105
Unfinished Business 106
"Tsunami" Days 108
Chapter 13: The Third Year and Beyond. 111
A Constant Companion. 111
The Lost Future. 113
The Real Future 113
Holding Memories 114
Staying Connected. 115
Transformation 116

Part 2: How to Help the Bereaved Mother. 119
Beyond the Imagination 121
Pitfalls to Avoid. 122
Key Support: Praise for Her Child 128
Provide Emotional Support. 131
Provide Spiritual Support 134
Provide Long-Term Support 136

Appendix: Resources for Bereaved Parents. 141
References. 145

Preface

THIS BOOK IS for two readers: bereaved mothers and those mothers' family and friends. Part 1 presents a practical, gentle survival manual for moms who have lost a son or daughter of any age by any means. The format of short sections with sub-headings allows you to pick the issue that is most pressing for you today. Each topic includes "Messages for Moms," which list specific suggestions to help guide you in coping with this horrific tragedy. Turn to these sections as often as necessary, since different words may be helpful at different times. While some parts of this guide may also be useful to your husband or adult children, it was written for you, the mother. I've created various metaphors and images throughout the book to help in your healing. Research findings support many of the statements, as indicated in the references.

Part 2 is written for friends and family or anyone else who wants to help a grieving mother. Please consider giving this last section to your friends and family as early as possible. While others will not be able to begin to understand your loss, they *can* be guided in how best to support you.

My heart is with you as you travel this painful journey and move toward healing and peace.

Part 1: A Survival Guide for Mothers

Gentle Suggestions and Messages for Bereaved Moms

CHAPTER 1

The Unimaginable

Initial Shock

THE LOSS OF your child hits like a speeding locomotive, crushing your body and mind as well as your heart. Some mothers see the train coming and try to brace themselves; others get hit from behind without warning. Either way, such catastrophic loss is unthinkable, unimaginable, and unbelievable. We can account for the sequence of events and explain all that happened yet still feel as if we are in some kind of surreal nightmare. Like wounded gazelles, we initially function with a partial anesthesia of shock and disbelief, all the while still racked with the pain of loss. We move through the necessary motions of our days without remembering the details, but we always do so with a constant preoccupation with the precious image of our children. This numbness is common in bereavement, and will lessen slowly over the months to come (Wing, Clance, Burge-Callaway & Armistead, 2001).

The catastrophic loss of a child is often incapacitating. In the immediate months, imagine yourself in an intensive care unit. If you were physically injured, you would only expect yourself to breathe and would slowly allow your body to heal. Try to give yourself the same permission now. Although your wounds are invisible, they are no less real. Drastically lower your expectations of yourself; give yourself a chance to simply comprehend this loss. If you can sit upright and take fluids and appropriately respond to others for the first few months, you are doing well!

I expected far too much of myself in the first few weeks following the loss of my own daughter, Melissa. Like the victim of a land mine who has not yet realized she has lost her legs, I was unaware of how difficult every movement would be in the initial weeks. I needed permission to do nothing, help with setting realistic expectations, and protection from overextending myself. No one could advise me, because our wounds are invisible to those who love us, since those around us are also injured and debilitated.

The age of the child at his or her time of death is irrelevant to a mother. (The word *child* in this book refers to your daughter or son at whatever age and developmental stage of life or adulthood he or she lived to reach.) A child of five minutes or fifty years is still your child and is still just as precious and irreplaceable. The more years with the child you were able to spend, the more haunted with all the memories and experiences you will be; the fewer years you spent with the child, the more cheated you will feel by the loss of the future happiness that was promised to you. Thus, *every* mother feels permanently bonded to her child and violently stripped of his or her future, regardless of the child's age. Whatever the circumstances, you are experiencing a catastrophic loss that will catapult you into a painful journey unlike any other experience you've ever had.

Each mother will have her own unique journey of grief and her own instinctive ways of healing. There are no rights or wrongs, no one way to experience loss or to heal. Honoring your *own* experiences and your *own* instincts is critical to your well-being. Use this guide in ways that may be helpful to you; ignore any content that does not apply to you. We all have different ways of healing (Pope, 2007; Thompson et al., 2011).

MESSAGES FOR MOMS: INITIAL SHOCK

ೞ **Avoid comparing yourself to anyone else. This is your journey to survive in whatever ways feel right for you.**

ೞ **Trust your instincts. Your inner voice will guide you with each step that is right for you.**

Rhythms of Grief

We usually experience our mourning in waves, not stages. We feel a mixture of intense emotions that tumble and fall together; different feelings will surface at different times, but they will often be intertwined. We may not detect any change in the intensity of the pain for many months or even until the second year after our loss. Initially, our lives will feel like an endless monsoon: a downpour of anger, longing, anxiety, and heartache. The thunderstorm of grief will overcome us with drowning rain for long periods of time before lessening a bit before the next wave of rainfall. As we slowly heal, the periods of clearing will become more frequent and longer, the downpours a bit less intense and shorter. In this way, our grieving will cycle like stormy weather for the years to come, gradually easing into more cycles of sunshine between more gentle rainfalls. Over time, the freedom to think about something else will become easier and more frequent. Expect the downpours to keep coming, but know that they will eventually be less fierce than they are today. You will heal, but the progress may be too subtle for you to detect at any one time. Below are a few suggestions for coping with these waves.

MESSAGES FOR MOMS: RHYTHMS OF GRIEF

ଔ **Every downpour is eventually followed by a time of clearing. Accept the times of being overcome by grief, knowing that you will feel better again eventually.**

ଔ **Focus on the spots of sunshine as they eventually break through to you. Savor the moments when you feel life is more "normal," which will come eventually.**

ଔ **Have patience with yourself during the thunderstorms of grief, allowing yourself the time and space to heal. Your distress expresses your immeasurable love for your child! Every tear honors this precious person whom you brought into your life.**

The Pain of Loss

The longing to see, hear, feel, and hold our children is excruciatingly intense and initially unrelenting: this is the pain of maternal grief. Such agonizing yearning is a result of our love for our children as well as our devotion to them. Our grief honors our children as a precious entity in this world, without whom the world would never be the same. As the months go by, we also grow to express our love in other ways. Initially, crying may be the only thing we can do.

We are organically wired to identify pain as negative: an indication that something is wrong with us. The intensity of this painful yearning can be terrifying to us. We find ourselves thrust into frightening and uncharted waters. Try to remember that every other mother who has lost a child has also traveled through this pain and has survived. You will, too.

Grief pain is an automatic and natural process; it is an outcome of your innate bond with the child whom you nurtured. An athlete in training experiences muscle aches as she builds her strength; a woman in labor experiences pain as her body works to open the birth canal. Both examples illustrate appropriate pain: hurt that is also part of a natural process. Your grief pain also works in a beneficial way, this time to widen your heart. As you allow yourself to process your loss and experience the emotional pain, your empathy for others will multiply without you even being aware of it. In birthing labor, the more the woman relaxes and works with the pain, the faster the work progresses. In grieving, accept this painful yearning as an inevitable part of the process that will aid your healing—and perhaps even your growth—in personal strength and compassion. Avoid the urge to fight the pain or bury the pain. Relax into the pain, and release it by expressing your agony in any way you can. Here are a few suggestions for releasing some of the pain you are experiencing.

MESSAGES FOR MOMS: THE PAIN OF LOSS

- ☞ **We must cry, both often and hard. Tears let out the pain and make room for healing. Some moms find that being alone and out of earshot helps to make them feel free to really let out the pain with sobs or even screams. Give yourself permission to cry or grieve in any way your heart tells you to do as often as you want to do so. Although feeling the intensity of your grief will be excruciating, you will experience an easing of your suffering once the crying is over.**

- ☞ **Process your feelings aloud with understanding souls. Find at least two or three people who can listen to your grief. As you cope with an unfamiliar level of distress, being able to think aloud with supportive people can be extremely helpful. Most mothers need to talk about their grief with someone, and they heal better when they process their feelings out loud with an understanding heart (Arnold & Gemma, 2008; Harper, O'Connor & O'Carrol, 2014).**

- ☞ **Consider looking beyond your immediate friends to other sources of support, such as parent-bereavement groups, social workers, members of the clergy, therapists, or other professionals affiliated with hospice or grief-support networks. The more people who support you, the more *effectively* your needs** will be met. Every bereaved mother *deserves* as much support as possible.

ᘓ If you know of another mom who has lost a child, consider talking to her. Although this is a vulnerable time for you when it will be more difficult to interact with new people, the right empathy from someone who has also lost a child can be incredibly helpful. Mothers who find this type of social support often experience fewer grief symptoms (Lepore, Silver, Wortman & Wayment, 1996).

ᘓ Consider contacting a mother from a bereaved-parent group or attending a meeting of such a group. A list of resources is included in the end of this book. Several studies have found that bereaved mothers reported receiving the most comfort from other mothers who have lost a child (Bouckaert, 2000; Cacciatore & Bushfield, 2007; Hunt & Greeff, 2011-2012; Nikkola, Kaunonen & Aho, 2013).

ᘓ Try to record, blog, journal, or express your pain in any way that feels right to you. Writing, drawing, or verbalizing your feelings will often help you to release them and to think about other positive things. Other bereaved parents recommend talking about your pain in e-mails, websites, or blogs (Thompson et al., 2011).

ᘓ Avoid falling into the habit of turning to alcohol or other substances to numb the pain. Seek professional help right away if you are tempted in this area. If you are experiencing distressing insomnia, anxiety, or depression, consult your doctor as soon as possible.

ଔ Internet or online support groups for bereaved parents have been helpful to some mothers, especially if no local support groups are available. Parents have reported the benefits of round-the-clock access for emotional support and the safety to talk about taboo subjects, thus making it easier to share their feelings or experiences (Elder & Burke, 2015; Feigelman, Gorman, Beal & Jordan, 2008).

Common Physical Reactions

Mothers often experience physical symptoms with their loss that are both very real and very normal. Catastrophic loss is traumatic not only to our hearts but also to our bodies and minds. Mothers most commonly experience insomnia and anxiety similar to posttraumatic shock reactions. Our minds work so hard at trying to comprehend this unimaginable loss that it makes sleeping difficult (Buckley et al., 2012; Miles, 1985; Murphy, Johnson & Lohan, 2003; Utz, Caserta & Lund, 2011).

We may feel anxious without knowing why. The floor of our lives has collapsed beneath us: we assumed that our child would outlive us, and that core belief is now shattered. We automatically move into a kind of hyperalert phase in which we unconsciously brace ourselves for another surprise attack. In the months following our loss, for example, my husband and I used to find each other in the kitchen in the middle of the night; at other times, we would look into our daughter's room and unconsciously expect her to be there. All this is normal, albeit stressful and painful. Your brain is simply struggling to comprehend the unthinkable.

Many mothers experience common physical symptoms of stress: loss of appetite or food cravings, back pain or headaches, and hormonal changes that result in an erratic menstrual cycle or hot flashes. Some mothers feel shortness of breath, a tightness in the throat, or a heaviness in the chest; some may occasionally be nauseous or gripped with fear (Bonanno & Kaltman, 2001; Kowalski & Bondmass, 2008; Stroebe, Schut & Stroebe, 2007; Wing et al., 2001).

Any physical discomfort can be related to your intense sorrow; our bodies and minds are interwoven and inseparable. The extreme stress of grief places us more at risk for colds or common infections and even accidents because we are so distracted. Our bodies are simply run-down from the enormous stress of loss (Buckley et al., 2012; Spratt & Denny, 1991).

Fatigue accompanies almost all loss and stays much longer than anticipated (Hunt & Greeff, 2011-2012; Stroebe et al., 2007). Your body and mind channel all your energy into processing this terrible loss. Just as a broken bone needs a cast or brace to heal, your body and mind need rest to recover physically and cognitively from this trauma. Some moms find that they need naps or perhaps a "rest day" at least weekly. In the weeks following the loss of my daughter, friends would call up and offer a supportive invitation to go for a walk with them. My feet felt like lead, and my usual pace was absolutely impossible. I did not have the energy for my usual activities the first few months. Chores piled up around me, since even the smallest effort seemed too much. One normally athletic mom said she could not walk to the end of the driveway to retrieve the mail; another mom needed months before she could return to her employment. (Both bereaved mothers referenced here were people I know, as are other examples in this book). Such physical fatigue is common and is to be expected.

MESSAGES FOR MOMS: COMMON PHYSICAL REACTIONS

- ❧ **Be patient with yourself. Try to accept whatever reaction your body has as part of your own healing journey. Many of these reactions are common to mothers who have lost a child.**

- ❧ **Listen to your body's cues. Give yourself the same permission to rest as if you had the flu. Your fatigue is real. You will return to a more normal functioning, but it may take months.**

- ❧ **Get help wherever you can. Ask close friends or family members for a hand, or hire a cleaning service for a few months and use take-out food services to lower the demands on you. Research shows that bereaved parents encourage one another to rely on outside help and advise one another to accept all offers from friends and neighbors (Thompson et al., 2011).**

- ❧ **Try to maintain your nutrition and normal self-care activities as much as you can. Avoid alcohol or unnecessary medications.**

ɔʒ   Try to sleep seven to eight hours a day, even if it is broken sleep. A sleep medication may be helpful in the short term to allow you to keep functioning; such medications are best taken under the guidance of your physician or nurse practitioner.

ɔʒ   Lessen the demands and obligations on you as much as possible. Exterior stress compounds all grief symptoms. If you are employed outside the home, take off as much time as possible that feels right to you. Research has suggested that having time to heal without having to deal with the demands of work can be very helpful to bereaved mothers (Sundell, 1998).

ɔʒ   For all physical symptoms, seek medical attention for any significant changes or any reactions that may indicate illness. The extreme stress of grief can result in real pathology, so no symptom should be dismissed.

Common Cognitive Reactions

Preoccupation with our lost loved one is the hallmark of all grief. Often a person in grief will fear that she is going crazy because her mind is so distracted and distressed. As our brains work harder and harder to process this loss, our mental acuity for other areas will be automatically lessened. Because our ability to concentrate becomes compromised, we forget why we walked into a room. We do not remember conversations we had or things we did. We lose track of important dates.

We misplace things more easily. One mom got so tired of losing her keys that she finally put them on a lanyard around her neck—a great example of just accepting the new reality of her life and making helpful adjustments. Distraction and inability to concentrate is normal and unavoidable, as many research studies have shown (Bonanno & Kaltman, 2001; Stroebe et al., 2007; Toblin et al., 2012; Utz et al., 2011).

MESSAGES FOR MOMS: COMMON COGNITIVE REACTIONS

- ⋙ **Try to accept that lack of focus is a normal reaction to loss that no one can control. You will regain your ability to think clearly, but it will take months and will return slowly.**

- ⋙ **Make lists, write things down, and stick to routine places for important things. Give yourself credit for accomplishing any cognitive task in the months following a catastrophic loss. Most people can only halfway function in a fog of automatic actions; this automation allows their brains to concentrate their energy on the necessary healing.**

- ⋙ **When your mind refuses to stay focused on the task at hand, give in to your memories of your child. Often when we take time to remember, honor, and painfully process the loss, we slowly gain longer periods when we are able to focus on something else.**

- ⋙ **Lower your expectations of yourself. Give yourself credit for breathing and getting out of bed every** day. If you are drinking healthy fluids, responding to others, making appropriate decisions, and wearing matching shoes, you are coping extremely well, no matter how much you cry or sleep!

ভ Look at what you *are* doing in the aftermath of catastrophic loss, rather than what you are unable to do right now. Each little action takes great effort, since your body and mind are struggling to heal from this trauma. You are carrying around a huge boulder of grief in addition to the weight of your daily routine. No one can go back to functioning at the same level we were previously until the weight of that grief lessens, which takes more time than we want to give. Just like healing a bone, healing from grief cannot be hurried. You have to accept the limits of the "cast" and allow your body and mind to heal in their own time.

Hunger and Yearning for Your Child

The intense longing for your child causes difficult emotional pain and unremitting agony. Our bodies and minds cry out deep from our core to see, hear, touch, smell, and feel our children. Although there is no way to satisfy these needs, bereaved mothers find many ways to stay connected to their lost children and recommend doing so to other bereaved mothers. Parents report a lessening of the intensity of their grief when they remain connected to their children and continue bonding practices for many years—usually their entire lifetime. For the bereaved parent, the goal of grief is not to cut your bond with your child, but to integrate your child as a spiritual presence in your life in a new way (Arnold & Gemma, 2008; Barrera et al., 2009; Klass, 1997; Thompson et al., 2011).

For many parents, their child has left this world to enter another world. Thus, their child still lives and continues to exist, but in a spiritual realm. For the purposes of this book, I refer to your child's physical death or earthly death, in order to make a distinction between their earthly life and their afterlife. Thus, at times I refer to your children in present tense, since their spirits still continue.

Here are a few ideas from other mothers who have survived this journey. When you are ready, some of these may bring you comfort.

MESSAGES FOR MOMS: HUNGER AND YEARNING

- ೞ Consider putting clothes worn by your child that still hold his or her body scent in a plastic bag to preserve the scent. I used to bury my head in a sweater my daughter had recently worn and would just breathe in the smell of her whenever I longed for her.

- ೞ Consider keeping some of your child's belongings near you. I use my daughter's key chain, for example, and wear several of her jackets. For adult children, ask their spouses for some of these belongings.

- ೞ I found looking at photos was one way that I could stop crying, although some parents cannot look at photos at all in the beginning. If and when pictures do comfort you, collect all the photos you can from others as well. Display and organize them in ways that will allow you to soak them up frequently and easily and as often as you desire.

ભ Consider listening to audio and video recordings of your child. Put these recordings in formats and electronic devices that you can easily access and absorb. Some moms have the last voice-mail messages from their children on their phones, which they play back frequently.

ભ If it comforts you, soak up your child's handwriting or artwork or other creations. I found my daughter's prayer journal in her drawer, and I copied her handwriting in order to make copies of quotes for her friends. I found tracing her letters and seeing how she formed words very soothing.

ભ Consider spending time in your children's space: their rooms, their offices or homes, their cars. Being where they spent time is another way of feeling closer. Visiting meaningful locations is a common way of continuing the bond for bereaved parents.

ભ Perhaps write down the happy memories as they come to you, or narrate your voice over a PowerPoint with photos once you have the energy to do so. Capturing the happy moments by reviewing them in your memory in any way possible keeps them close to your heart. Journaling in any form is also therapeutic.

- ଔ Parents often establish rituals or habits that remind them of their children and help them feel connected, such as continuing an activity they did together or an activity that they loved (Norton & Francesca, 2014).

- ଔ Create an Internet memorial or a Facebook page.

- ଔ Give yourself permission to comfort your longing in any way that works for you for as long as you need to do so. Ignore the voices in your head or your family members or friends who push you to "move on." By allowing yourself to process your grief, you *are* moving on and healing, even if no one else understands. Bereaved parents continue the bond with their children by remembering, loving, and caring and often recommend that other bereaved parents try to do the same (Arnold & Gemma, 2008).

How Do I Go On?

No mother wants to think about life without her child. The longing to see our son or daughter again is far more intense than anyone can anticipate, the agony more excruciating. We know we will not see, touch, or hear our child's physical presence again, and such a thought seems intolerable. We are in the intensive care unit wondering, "How can I endure life in this state?" We fear that the pain will never end. One mother might wish for her own death soon after her loss, while another may fear death; both are normal reactions. A logical response to wanting to be with your child is to go where she is: in this case, the afterlife. For most moms, this is *not* contemplating suicide but simply wanting to be somewhere else that is less painful. Avoid adding needless guilt to these normal feelings (Harper, O'Connor, Dickson & O'Carroll, 2011).

In the months following my loss, I would comfort myself with the knowledge that I might die in two or three years from some disease. Although I wanted my surviving child to be cared for well, I found comfort in thinking that I might not have too much longer to live until I would again be with my daughter in heaven. Entertaining the possibility of a shorter life not only eased my sorrow but helped me make more use of each day. As the thunderstorms of grief began to ease into alternating gentle rain and sunshine, my desire to continue with my earthly life grew stronger and my thoughts of death ceased. If you find yourself longing to be with your child, ask yourself: What do you want to do for your loved ones before you die? Who are you caring for now on this earth who needs you? Focus on giving to these loved ones who are here with you while you still can.

Although we anticipate that the years ahead of us spent without our children will be intolerable, we will heal eventually. We recover our balance in life, even though we will always be missing a piece of our lives. We do regain our ability to laugh, to be productive, to help others, and even to enjoy parts of our lives. If this is impossible for you to imagine right now, than remember that you only have today to live.

MESSAGES FOR MOMS: GOING ON

☘ **Take one day at a time. You do not need to survive forever. Just today.**

ಯ Focus on caring for yourself and doing something for your loved ones who are around you now whenever you can. They need you more than ever.

ಯ If you can, give yourself permission to take a "break" from your grief. Go to the movies or go away for a weekend, if either of those appeal to you.

ಯ Your reaction to your loss is normal and unique to you. No one can predict your response or give you an exact prescription for healing. Your instincts will guide you. Trust them.

CHAPTER 2

Anger, Guilt, Envy, and Anxiety

Anger

PAIN CAN MAKE us angry; this is often an automatic human response. Following catastrophic loss, we may experience anger ranging from occasional moments of irritation to constant and intense rage. We may be intolerant of irritable events, inconveniences, and flaws in others. Our patience may leave us. We may have short fuses that are easily set off by daily frustrations.

It is all too common to become consumed with rage by such tragedies. We use our justified outrage to target anyone who might be to blame for the loss. For those of you who have lost a child suddenly, you may experience many different compounding injuries on top of your loss: hurtful publicity, legal stresses, and confrontations with an actual criminal. The severe emotional ordeals that can hit you are beyond description. Of course, you are irate and suffering indescribable pain (Arnold & Gemma, 2008; Feigelman, Jordon & Gorman, 2009; Wijngaards-de Meij et al., 2008).

Anger is far more culturally and socially accepted than open sorrow. Friends can handle hearing our rage about our loss but will crumble at witnessing our unveiled distress. Many people fear our intense mourning, since they'll feel helpless and incapable of responding, but they'll be able to listen to and agree with our anger. We find social acceptance and reinforcement of anger but not of our deepest anguish.

Anger is a safer expression of our immense pain that protects us from the full force of the grief. Our rage covers our distress like a scab on a wound. As long as we are consumed with anger, we keep the real deepest suffering suppressed with the fire of rage. Anger is a normal reaction, but it fails to help us heal. Such a consuming inferno does little than to devour and destroy us in the process. Anger eats away our inner core and strength by blocking healing and devastating any hope of attaining peace. No matter how justified it is, our anger wreaks havoc on our well-being.

Since anger keeps us from feeling the full intensity of our loss, we hang onto it. We fuel it with justifications that are real and valid but *not* helpful to our health. In order to stop the destructive force of our anger, we need to confront the full impact of our loss. When I gave myself time and permission to touch the full depth of my grief and express it with uncontrolled tears or wails, my anger disappeared for a while. After I acknowledged and thoroughly expressed my intense grief, I found more emotional energy and space to focus on the positive things in my life. The anger was a way of keeping the pain under control. Once I released the pain, I could let go of the anger and choose to focus on the positive parts of what was left of my life. After releasing the pain appropriately with tears, I became calmer and less irritable with my other family members. Being irritable and grumpy always signals my need to take time to feel my loss and express my grief in some way.

MESSAGES FOR MOMS: ANGER

- ⊗ Vent your anger in safe ways: write in a journal and rant and rave at God, the right friend, therapist, or a clergy member, but don't rant and rave at your immediate family members.

- ⊗ Accept that you have no patience with others right now and that this is OK. You will someday regain your normal sunny disposition. In the meantime, try to limit the damage by staying out of difficult situations or leaving the scene when people irritate you.

- ⊗ Let others know that your anger or irritability is really your distress about your loss. When I found myself snapping at my family members, I would go back and explain to them: "It's really just my grief. I'm sorry." Try to let your close family know that they are not the cause of your real misery; this will be a huge factor in preserving those precious relationships. People can often forgive you for almost anything if they know that whatever it was wasn't their fault.

- ⊗ Forgive family members for their anger. Try to remember that they are coping the best they can. When they are irritable and bickering, see the pain behind their irritation. Whatever issues they are angry about are acting as smoke screens. The source of all real pain for each of you is the loss of your precious child.

   ᙍ   **Find positive ways to grieve. Create remembrances for your child with photos, websites, or belongings. Some moms find physical exercise, walking, yoga, or a massage to be a healthy release of negative energy.**

   ᙍ   **Once you have expressed your pain, try to look for the little things you can be grateful for: photos, the years and memories you have with your child, the support you are receiving now. We must express our sorrow, but we may also choose to focus our perspective on the positive as much as possible. Research suggests that parents who turn their focus on doing positive things for others in honor of their children experience lessened grief intensity (Harper et al., 2014).**

Guilt

Some primal instinct deep in your core tells you that you failed as a mother in allowing your child to die. Such guilt is completely irrational but often unavoidable, regardless of the type of death it was. Many mothers feel this instinctive guilt no matter how unfounded or unjustified it is. One mom wondered if she had taught her thirtysomething daughter how to cross a road properly after she had been killed crossing the street in broad daylight by a reckless driver. Since her daughter had been successfully living an independent adult life in a large city for many years, obviously this mom had done a wonderful job teaching her safety skills. The question was illogical but inescapable for this woman. We cling to an unconscious assumption that we can protect our children from disaster, and that core belief gets shattered by the death of a child. We automatically jump to the conclusion that "this must somehow be my fault." For some mothers, circumstances give them more room to find fault with themselves: "I should have taken her to the doctor sooner," or "I should have been firmer with his curfews." These tormenting questions are often unavoidable and are commonly termed the "should've, could've, would've" processes. These "if onlys" are inevitable regardless of circumstances, and they torture us with the least amount of rational justification. Each of these thoughts may viciously haunt and torment those parents who experience sudden death by accident or violence (Arnold & Gemma, 2008; Duncan & Cacciatore, 2015; Hunt & Greeff, 2011-2012; Barr, 2012).

In addition to whatever blame or mistakes we may accuse ourselves of in relation to the death, we will also replay events throughout the child's life that we subsequently regret. We all make mistakes in parenting, some of which will be blaring to us in retrospect. The child's earthly death will bring up our past regrets and failures with penetrating sharpness.

Each of the "if only" thinking pathways are destructive to us. We want to control every situation and be perfect every time, but no one can do that. Just as we struggle to come to terms with our children's mortality, so must we also accept our own frailty and imperfections.

MESSAGES FOR MOMS: GUILT

 CB **Try to limit your "if only" thoughts. We have to *choose* to not go there. When we begin to think, "if only," we need to tell ourselves that "these thoughts** are not helpful." Try to turn your focus on something you did well for your child instead.

ೞ If you forgive your loved ones for their mistakes—in other words, if you forgive them for being human beings—then you must also forgive yourself. Your child would want you to forgive yourself! Choose forgiveness.

ೞ Whatever you did, your actions and words were the best you could do at that time. Tell yourself, "I did the best I could, which is all anyone can do."

ೞ Focus on ways you *were* successful as a mother! Rather than looking at the 5 percent of the time you wish you had done more, look at the 95 percent of the time when you did everything that you could do! Post reminders of ways you were a "good" mom to focus your thoughts on the positive.

ೞ Get input from others whom you trust who can reinforce you as a mother; family members are best, but a good friend or counselor may also be helpful in identifying all the ways you are a "good" mom.

ೞ Seek support from parents whose children have died in the same way. Parents who are confronted with suicide often find powerful help with support groups for parents who have lost children in the same kinds of tragedies. Parents who experience sudden death of any kind often find self-help parent groups especially beneficial (Thrift & Coyle, 2005; Schwab, 1996).

ଔ   Self-forgiveness is a spiritual exercise. If you believe that God forgives, then you must forgive yourself as well. If possible, allow your faith beliefs, practices, and/or your faith community to be a support to you in reassuring you that you are forgiven.

ଔ   This is an individual journey. Be patient and rely on the support of other helpful people who love you, other moms who have walked this same journey, and your spiritual worldview. Ultimately, most moms do find peace through the journey.

Envy

Most of us envy other mothers who have not gone through this loss, even though we would never, ever wish such a catastrophe on anyone else. Envy is part of the normal feelings of "Why me?" We see other mothers with their children and ache to be in their places: a whole family. Watching other families do normal activities feels like salt in an open wound—a cruel reminder that our family is forever changed. Such reminders are everywhere and are simply part of the agony of the initial period following loss. Avoid adding guilt to this envy. Longing to have your child and family back is inevitable; wishing you still had your child is automatic. These are normal feelings that many bereaved mothers experience (Arnold & Gemma, 2008; Barr & Cacciatorre, 2007/2008).

As time goes on, others will forget your loss and will be unable to anticipate how their words and actions affect you. People may think that your interacting with their children will somehow ease the pain of losing your own when the opposite may in fact be true. Spending time with intact families who are playing and having fun may shine a spotlight on your loss. Others will be unaware that celebrating their children's milestones will only augment the loss of those milestones in your own life.

You need to protect yourself from situations that are especially painful and people who cannot understand what you are going through. One mother of a stillborn baby boy still refuses to ever attend baby showers for boys, even decades later and after having several daughters. Another mother who lost an adult daughter refuses to ever attend a wedding, since it would simply be too painful for her. We all have different social situations that trigger intense pain. The challenge is to anticipate especially difficult situations and stay firm in setting boundaries to protect ourselves from unnecessary heartache for as long as we feel the need to do so.

Messages for Moms: Envy

- ⋘ **Respect your feelings and your need to limit your exposure to other families' happy, normal occasions until, if, or when you are ready to emotionally participate. Taking several years to heal is common for mothers who have lost children.**

- ⋘ **Reassure your close family members that you will heal in time, but tell them that the first few years** will be especially difficult and that you will need extra consideration.

ᔥ Put your own need to heal first—put your needs above others' needs to have you join in their activities or events. Your wounds are invisible but real! You may not be able to make them understand, but they *can* respect and honor your choices.

ᔥ If you anticipate that you might be in a social situation that will bring intense grief, have an escape plan ready: a way to leave whenever you might need to do so.

Anxiety

In the weeks following my daughter's physical death, an urgent, emergency state came over my body. I felt like a civilian trapped in a basement in the midst of urban guerrilla fighting. I tensely waited for something else horrible to happen while I remained alert for the next bomb to hit. Bereaved mothers like me often find ourselves restless and unable to sit still and relax. Our sleeping is difficult. Our minds are constantly churning over the loss as we try to comprehend what has happened. Our bodies are filled with the tension of tragedy, even while we are exhausted. Indeed, the tension itself drains us of all energy. This common posttraumatic-stress type of reaction leaves us hyperalert and anxious (Cacciatore, Lacasse, Lietz & McPherson, 2013-2014; Duncan & Cacciatore, 2015; Mancini, Prati & Black, 2011; Murphy, 1999; Murphy, Johnson & Lohan, 2003).

MESSAGES FOR MOMS: ANXIETY

ଔ Accept your anxiety and restlessness as normal and know that these symptoms will decrease over time. The more we are distressed by our grief symptoms, the more we fuel them.

ଔ Focus on the positives in your life right now. As crazy as it may sound, some moms find it helpful to keep a "gratitude journal" in which they list the little positive comforts or words that get them through the day. The mental discipline of focusing on the positive redirects your thoughts away from the disaster in your life and strengthens your coping skills (Sin & Lyubomirsky, 2009). Bereaved parents often recommend trying to cherish the good moments of today (Thompson et al., 2011).

ଔ Meditation, prayer, guided imagery, and slow, deep breathing are all effective for some people. For example, take a deep breath in and exhale to a very slow count of five. Repeat a few times and feel your muscles relax. Ten minutes a day of prayer or meditation can also be hugely helpful.

ଔ Physical activity of any type will help relieve some of your tension: walks, yoga, swimming, or any other movement that feels comforting.

ଔ Routine activities such as folding laundry or washing dishes can also be soothing. Doing something that feels a part of normal, daily life reassures us of some consistency.

ℂ℥ A hot bath before bedtime or a professional massage or pedicure may help. Even rubbing your own feet or stroking your scalp can be soothing.

ℂ℥ For some people, sports, hobbies, or other creative activities serve as a good way to release tension.

ℂ℥ Combine multiple strategies for stress relief, and use them consistently in your daily schedule.

ℂ℥ Give yourself permission to seek objective, professional consultation and support if your anxiety is distressing to you. Seeking help appropriately is a positive coping strategy.

When patients experience physical pain, nurses may use hand massage or a back rub to decrease the pain in other parts of the body. The pleasurable sensations of the warm, soothing touch compete with the pain stimulus and will actually slightly diminish the perception of the physical pain. In the same way, fill your life with as many soothing physical sensations and as much positive thinking as you can. You are countering your body's shock state with calming thoughts and stimuli to regain your sense of balance and control in the world. You will slowly become less anxious as you heal.

CHAPTER 3

Triggers and Holidays

Triggers

"TRIGGERS" ARE THE sights, words, and events in our surroundings and daily activities that touch our grief and bring it to the surface in uncontrollable ways. Triggers can be memorabilia, places, objects, songs, people, or anything that brings back memories. Although the constant presence of grief is inescapable in the first months, an intensified sorrow can dissolve even the most fortified of us into a puddle of tears. Often moms can better forgive themselves for public outbursts or incapacitating emotional pain when they can identify the trigger: the event or circumstances that caused the exacerbated response of grief. Each mom will have many and different triggers, but some of these triggers are very common (Hunt & Greeff, 2011-2012).

Grocery stores can bring back the memories of all the ways you took care of your child by buying her food. One mom simply changed the supermarket she used, never again returning to those familiar aisles where she had picked up packages just for her son. Other places may remind you of fun you had with your child or of the last time you did things together. Even the most ordinary sight can bring up memories and intense pain.

Avoiding distressing triggers whenever possible is a healthy way to cope with loss. Give yourself permission to change food markets, vacation spots, daily traffic patterns, or whatever else it may be that feels too painful to you. Alternatively, give yourself permission to frequent familiar places that *do* comfort you and give you the feeling of being closer to your child. Some moms need to completely avoid certain triggers to remain functional, whereas other moms may crave being in those places to soak up the memories. Do what feels right for you!

People can also be triggers for your loss. You may know people whom you feel were unkind to your child or who bring up negative memories for other reasons. Sometimes, a few well-intentioned kind words from a good friend can hit you the wrong way and bring up deep grief. Seeing someone who is the same age your child was, or who is in a similar situation, can bring tears. All these reactions are normal and will ease with time.

MESSAGES FOR MOMS: TRIGGERS

ᔆ **Allow yourself freedom to feel whatever you are feeling. Our emotions are part of who we are and cannot be controlled. What we *do* with our emotions, and how we handle our feelings, will determine constructive coping (or healing) versus destructive coping (becoming bitter and resentful).**

ᔆ **Accept that your grief is normal and uncontrollable and your reactions to triggers unavoidable.**

ᘓ   Give yourself space and time to heal, and give your-
     self permission to avoid triggers as needed.

ᘓ   If you are concerned about a social situation, have
     an escape plan ready in case you find your grief is
     suddenly triggered and becomes uncontrollable.

ᘓ   Take time and find ways to express and release
     your pain in some of the healthy ways suggested in
     chapter 1.

The Grave

Many mothers hold intense feelings about their children's
earthly remains. Some mothers need to be near them daily.
Some mothers cannot bear the reminder of the grave site for
many years. All reactions are normal and need to be honored.

Every decision surrounding the ashes, grave site, and
stone may seem monumental. I remember looking at stones
for my daughter's grave site barely two months after her
passing, which may have been too soon. My own mother
was anxious to have the grave marked and kept asking me
about the progress, which added to the pressure I felt. When
I received the drawings in the mail four months later, I calmly
studied the plans and analytically looked at the spacing and
details before putting it away. I thought I was handling it
very well until I tried to go to sleep that night, which was
impossible. Sometimes our expression of mourning comes
out unconsciously in our actions or bodily responses. I was so
frightened by how easily this trigger made me less functional

that I put away the plans until six months later, when I had a week's vacation from my work. It was a full two years before we had a stone on my daughter's grave, but I was satisfied with the outcome.

MESSAGES FOR MOMS: THE GRAVE

- ℭ Take all the time you need to make decisions about any memorials for your child. For many of us, these decisions are highly stressful and need to be spread out over time.

- ℭ Don't allow others to pressure you into making decisions before you are ready; fit the design or content to whatever feels right to you. No one else has a right to dictate these decisions other than the immediate family: you, the father, and/or the spouse of your child.

- ℭ Give yourself credit for being able to think about this heavy decision at all! Seeing your child's name on a grave marker or urn is traumatic. Give yourself credit for bearing such pain and accomplishing this task—no matter how long it takes.

- ℭ Visit the grave site or crematorium as often or infrequently as you desire. There are no rules. Trust your inclinations. Some moms spend a whole day, while others cannot bear to visit at all. Everyone is different. You will know when you need to be there.

⍳ **Honor the grave site as you wish within the rules of the cemetery, such as with plantings. Know that you have years ahead of you when you can do this, and give yourself the freedom to change from year to year.**

Your Child's Belongings

You are likely to have strong attachment to at least some, if not all, of your child's belongings: his clothes, possessions, mementos, or anything that he used or loved. Such things can offer helpful comfort in feeling closer to your child. You may also feel pressure to "move on" and let go of your child's belongings. We live in a culture that does not accept what is normal for grieving parents: the lifelong feelings of loss. Most people in Western culture still believe that the healthiest way to deal with grief will result in "closure": a point where one actually stops thinking about or missing the person. Grieving parents and social scientists alike now know that the "normal" bereavement of a parent for a child is never over, even though parents eventually heal from the devastation and recover enough to live rewarding lives. Parents will always miss their children, always long for them, always carry them in their hearts. Hanging on to your child's belongings facilitates this healthy, ongoing attachment and remembrance of your child. These tangible links to your child provide a useful way to stay connected, thereby comforting your longing (Arnold & Gemma, 2008; Barrera et al., 2009; Harper et al., 2011; Hunt & Greeff, 2011-2012; Klass, 1997; Thompson et al., 2011).

If your child was no longer living at home, you might not have access to his or her belongings. You can stay connected to your child in many ways: through memories, photos, places, routines, and traditions. Even substitute, look-alike objects can serve as the tangible symbol of your child.

MESSAGES FOR MOMS: YOUR CHILD'S BELONGINGS

    ʗ**If circumstances permit, avoid giving away or throwing away your child's possessions too hastily. If you need them out of sight, ask someone to pack them away temporarily. You have years ahead of you to empty out closets. Some parents find those possessions important years later, since grief does change over time. One mom sewed a quilt from her child's favorite clothes, but not until years after her loss. You may need several years to even begin to think clearly about your child's possessions.**

    ʗ**Spend whatever time you need to with these possessions. I found I did not want to go away on vacation for the first few months of my loss, because being in my own home was comforting to me. Other moms need to change their homes or move completely. Any response is correct as long as you follow your heart.**

    ʗ**Ignore any hints from others that you should be doing something different with your child's possessions. Only *you* will know what you need for comforting your heart. Only another parent who has gone** through loss can appreciate what these possessions mean to you or guess at the extent of your pain.

Ↄ Mothers should keep the most meaningful of their children's possessions easily accessible, if that provides comfort to them. Wear their clothes or jewelry, display their artwork, or play with their sports equipment.

Ↄ Maintain your child's room intact as long as you wish. One mom moved with her family a year after her son's earthly death. She not only set up her son's room in her new home but kept her son's clothes in their original drawers. She was able to leave the house in which her child had lived by keeping her son's possessions and presence in her new home. She said her friends who had helped her pack tacitly disapproved of her actions, but she bravely and wisely ignored their discomfort.

Ↄ Give yourself permission to replace items that remind you of your missing child. During Victorian times, people commonly had jewelry made with locks of hair from their deceased loved ones. Do whatever feels comforting for *you*.

Holidays and Family Events

Any occasion that your family used to mark as "family get-together time" will likely trigger your grief. Even the anticipation of such an event months ahead of time may cause anxiety and insomnia or other grief symptoms. Thanksgiving and Christmas were clearly tough days for my family. Our first Thanksgiving, we had a great excuse for not attending my sister's dinner as usual. The day didn't feel like Thanksgiving, which was a relief. Unfortunately, extended family members may think they can "cheer you up" and "help you forget" your sorrow for that day, which will just add to the feelings of isolation and loneliness you may experience. Mothers commonly feel angry when their children are excluded from family gatherings and their names or very existence no long acknowledged during any interactions in the course of such events (Klass, 1997). Sometimes we have to be clear and adamant about what we need for holiday celebrations, which is extremely difficult to do in such a vulnerable state as grief for the loss of a loved one. You are the one who has lost a child, not your siblings or parents. Your needs come first for at least the first few years—if not always.

For major family holidays, try to talk about your plans for the holidays as an immediate family. Everyone is anticipating (or dreading) the same thing: the first family holiday without your child. Find out your spouse/partner's and surviving children's preferences and negotiate the best you can. My surviving child wanted "everything the same" for Christmas, so that's what we did.

Acknowledging your child in some way during the holidays often helps to ease the pain. I hung an angel from our dining room light for the dinner table's centerpiece. I kept my daughter's Christmas stocking in the usual place and invited her friends and family to write notes to her that they would place in her stocking, although few did so. I also placed a favorite toy peeking out of the top in order to keep the stocking from looking so empty. I sent out the last photos of our family together that first Christmas, in that way keeping my daughter ever a part of our family. Other moms have gone away on vacation over the holidays with their surviving children, creating different memories or ignoring the holiday completely. How you survive the holidays will be different for each family. In time, you will eventually be able to enjoy such gatherings again, even though they will never be the same.

Less obvious holidays may bring up painful memories in surprising ways. For me, Halloween triggered memories of dressing up my child. All the anticipation and child activities of that holiday brought back the loss each year, even though she had long outgrown trick-or-treating by the time of her bodily death. Valentine's Day was always special to my daughter, both as a child and as a young woman. I thought I had gotten through the first Valentine's Day well. We did our usual family exchange at the dinner table, and I thought I was all right until I could not sleep at all that night. We cannot control our grief reactions, so we need to relax and let our bodies and minds heal with the time they need. When your physical symptoms of grief or forgetfulness emerge around the holidays, simply lower your expectations of yourself and know that this will pass.

For Christians, Easter and Holy Week often bring incredible pain. I struggled for years with this holiday, feeling guilty about my bereavement on the day that celebrates our ability to enter heaven. When I heard another woman who had lost her dad recount her resurgence of grief during Holy Week, I then realized that this was a common and normal response to a holiday that focuses on death and the afterlife. Just knowing other grieving people felt similar pain helped me accept my own feelings and modify my actions appropriately.

New Year's Eve brings direct contrast to our feelings. Everyone else is celebrating a holiday, while we are racked with pain that another year is arriving without our son or daughter. How can this be? My first New Year's was spent with close friends. As the ball dropped down, I wanted to let out a primal scream! Having to pretend and say "Happy New Year" just made my pain so much worse than it already was. My surviving child was at another party and had the identical reaction of intense grief at the stroke of midnight and burst out sobbing. We both were unprepared for the shock of pain that New Year's brought us.

For some families, Super Bowl Sunday or the Fourth of July may be excruciating. Family birthdays trigger intense feelings of loss, especially for the person who is celebrating the birthday. How can we have a family milestone without everyone there? How can I get older but not my child/sibling? Healthy ways to cope are to acknowledge the pain for yourself and your family members and reassure everyone that this is normal and will eventually lessen over time. The sadness may never completely go away, but it will become less intense.

Often we anticipate how awful a holiday will feel, and sometimes that anticipation is worse than the actual day turns out to be. Other times, we are caught completely off-guard, as I was on my first New Year's Eve without my daughter. We are all moving through uncharted waters. The best we can do is honor our feelings, remember that all this is normal and is experienced by most parents in grief, and trust that we will heal over time.

MESSAGES FOR MOMS: HOLIDAYS AND FAMILY EVENTS

ଔ   Allow each family member to cope in his or her own way. There is no one right way to heal.

ଔ   Try to offer flexibility, even with religious holidays. There may be a few years when your religious practices surrounding Good Friday or Passover may need to be altered to make room for your pain. You would not expect someone who is hospitalized to attend religious activities, for example. Although your wounds are invisible, they are no less real. You will know when and if you are ready to resume these activities.

ଔ   Talk about family gatherings ahead of time and plan ways to make them more enjoyable and comfortable for everyone. Think outside the box by suggesting new ways of celebrating for the first few years—or not celebrating at all.

ଔ   If you need to, avoid parties or large, happy celebrations on painful days, since often the contrast of your feelings with everyone else's cheerfulness will augment your loneliness. If you are uncertain and wish to attend a social gathering, be ready with an excuse to leave early if necessary, just in case your pain blocks your ability to enjoy the setting.

ಚ Integrate your child into the celebration: a picture on the table, a poem, a candle, or a symbol of his or her presence in the celebration. Parents commonly include such symbols of the spiritual presence of their children during celebrations for the rest of their lives.

ಚ Find ways to process the pain, and encourage your family members to do the same. For some, journaling or making art or talking to a close, trusted friend can provide a helpful outlet. Others release pain with intense workouts at the gym.

ಚ Rest! I found napping essential for handling the increased stress of holidays.

ಚ Focus on the positive in your life right now. Do what you can to reflect back the strengths to the important people who are now in your life who grieve with you. People in grief especially need positive feedback, which can be powerful in even the smallest of ways.

Your Child's Birthday

Your child's birthday can be especially difficult. Some moms find the birthday even more painful than the anniversary of the child's physical death. How inconceivable that this child you nurtured and raised could now be gone! Acknowledging the day in some way is important to many of us, since it gives expression to our sorrow. Honoring your child's birthday shows your love and gives due recognition to your loss.

The impact of the birthday spans more than a day, spilling into the weeks before and after the actual date. Our minds become consumed with normal preoccupations with our child's memory accompanied by your usual symptoms: whatever physical and cognitive changes you commonly experience with mourning. We need to accept this normal grieving process and set realistic expectations for ourselves.

Messages for Moms: Your Child's Birthday

- ❧ Discuss with your family members what their needs may be, which could be very different from yours. Many people wish to avoid such painful days by ignoring them and pretending it's just another day. Families need to show acceptance of differences among family members and provide forgiveness and freedom for each person to heal in his or her own way and time. Your surviving family members love your child as much as ever, even if their ways of honoring are very different, very private, and come with a different timeline.

- ❧ Allow others to support you and join with you in your honoring. Your friends and extended family members wish to support you. If your child had reached teen or adult age, his or her friends will be keenly remembering their birthday and may welcome an invitation to be with others who are also grieving. I found out years later that Melissa's friends get together for a dinner around her birthday as a remembrance to her. Providing space for such gathering and remembrances can be helpful to you as well.

❧ Draw on your traditions and extend them as you are comfortable. Many people have a Mass for their children on their birthdays and anniversaries.

❧ Use electronic means to honor your child. Some moms keep their children's Facebook pages active. Set up an e-mail list or a web space for comments. Perhaps send messages to all who knew your son or daughter and ask for them to share a few words to describe your child. Just seeing the positive words and knowing that people are remembering your child may be helpful.

❧ Establish rituals for remembering your child: not only on special days, but at any time.

❧ Some families invite others to join them in honoring the child's birthday. If you want such a gathering to be treated as a memorial, provide structure for remembering, and plan ahead about how you would like this time to be spent. Ask someone to read a poem, or share a memory, or share descriptions of your child. You might consider having someone serve as a leader to guide the time in a structured way that will clearly provide space for remembering and honoring. Perhaps have photos of your child or special objects on display. Ask people to write down their favorite things about your child on a card, and use these comments to start an open sharing of memories and thoughts. Although some people may be initially uncomfortable with this, your lead will help put the participants at ease. Wait until after your "remembering" time before serving any food or beverages, since such nourishment signals a more social occasion. The larger the gathering, the more structure and guidance will be necessary to provide for honoring your child. Without clear direction, your guests will default into social, "party" behavior, which may not be helpful to you.

ය Your needs to honor your child are important. Your friends and family need your guidance about how best to support you. The more you can be clear about your requests, the better they will be able to respond in a positive way.

Individual suggestions: You may also want to honor your child by yourself or just your family when marking birthdays and anniversaries. I know of one mother who baked a cake for her son's fortieth birthday, even though he had died decades earlier. It is never too late or inappropriate to connect with your child. Some ideas of activities that may comfort you may include

♥ lighting a candle;
♥ leaving flowers or plants at the grave site;
♥ visiting a place that your child loved;

- ♥ **reading one of your child's favorite books or stories;**
- ♥ **poring over their photos;**
- ♥ **cooking a favorite dish; or**
- ♥ **watching their favorite movie.**

Honoring our sons or daughters is a part of holding them in our hearts and is always an appropriate action for grieving parents in whatever way feels right.

CHAPTER 4

Loss: A Spiritual Crisis

How Can This Happen?

DISASTER HAS CRUELLY and unfairly struck down our cherished child, rendering us appropriately outraged. We are racked with existential questions: "How can this happen?" or "Why my child?" or even "How can there be a God who allows such suffering?"

Our world has been shattered by an inconceivable and irreparable loss. Whatever faith we had in a higher power is automatically challenged. Some moms reject the belief in any divine being. Some continue to rail against a world or a God that would allow such a thing to happen. Some moms eventually find peace with a new understanding. We all take our own journeys.

Focusing on the injustice that has been done to us can easily lead to self-pity. We naturally feel sorry for ourselves in the face of such intense pain. Our loss is extreme and tragic and our self-pity is completely justified, but it is not necessarily helpful to us. Such self-pity fuels destructive rage. The more we complain, rail, rebel, and pity ourselves, the further we are likely to sink into the muck and mire of anger and depression. Many people find that spiritual answers and religious beliefs help them from continuing to fall further into this misery (Arnold & Gemma, 2008; Bohannon, 1991; Wijngaards-de Meij et al., 2005).

Choose positive ways of coping. We can hang on to anger, wallow in self-pity, and end up with shriveled, bitter hearts, feeling cheated all our lives. Or, we can choose to accept the devastation of our loss slowly over time. We feel the pain and find ways to express it, knowing that our agony is one expression of our love. I would cry while also reminding myself that this is where I am supposed to be right now for reasons that I cannot understand. Such thinking allowed me to be honest with the extent of my injury while still avoiding the trap of self-pity.

How Could God Allow This?

Many of us direct our anger at God, whom we counted on to save our children and keep them safe. How could a loving God allow such a thing to happen? This existential question tortures us until we find an answer that we can accept, which is an individual journey that may take years.

If you are a person of faith, then talk to God. Scream, cry, and rant at God. Venting our anger at God can be helpful, therapeutic, and safe. God can handle our anger—the only One who will not take it personally or abandon us.

Many people need time to tackle these difficult questions. I found Jerry Sittser's 2004 book *A Grace Disguised: How the Soul Grows through Loss* to be helpful with existential questions but perhaps best read after the first few months.

The Faith Factor

Some mothers find comfort in their spiritual beliefs. For me, faith provided a path for healing. Rather than explain the inexplicable, my faith challenged me to trust a loving God, even though I could not understand how such tragedy could happen. Peace came not by learning why my daughter was taken but by knowing the God whom I trusted to be loving and good. Rather than stumble in the darkness of confusion, doubt, self-pity, and anger, I chose to cling to the gracious God I do know. My daughter believed that God took her "home" early to spare her from something worse. I choose to believe the same and remind myself that I am in this place of pain for some kind of good reason and purpose that I will someday understand. Faith is a choice. Our choices will direct our healing through every step of the process.

Whatever spiritual framework you find helpful, draw on it now, as many bereaved parents recommend (Thompson et al., 2011). Stay in dialogue with God. Rant, rave, scream, cry, question, and bring all your most passionate feelings to your Creator. God is the only One capable of handling the full intensity of our negative emotions, our questions, our fears, and our pain. You will see answers, often in unexpected ways. On my most painful days, God sent me special encouragements and reminders of His love. You will eventually gain some peace if you remain connected in dialogue with God.

Some moms instinctively turn to scripture or sacred writings for help. For Jewish or Christian mothers, the psalms give voice to our lament and heartache while also offering hope. Use any and all spiritual resources you have at your command to continue this journey and process, knowing that all this healing takes a long time.

Where Is My Child Now?

For bereaved mothers, knowing we will see our child again can be extremely helpful (Arnold & Gemma, 2008). Belief in an afterlife can make the difference between mourning the complete loss of the child or envisioning only a long separation. For me, trusting that my child is in a good place relieves my torment of wondering where she is, whether or not she exists, and if I will see her again. Because belief in an afterlife can be immeasurably helpful in limiting our suffering, I encourage mothers to explore their spiritual tendencies or inclinations in whatever ways are comfortable for them. Our healing journey is a spiritual pilgrimage.

Many mothers find comfort in some form of a traditional belief system or religion. Some moms find their own tradition a huge comfort, while others reject the beliefs of childhood to find more helpful spiritual nourishment in other traditions. Being with people of faith helps to nurture our own faith. Although you may have moved away from the practices of your childhood, now is a good time to explore your spiritual development and consider a faith community for your current needs. Our children are now spiritual beings. The more we connect and grow spiritually, the better we may find comfort with their new entity.

If you have been away from a faith community and now seek this support, begin with prayer for guidance in finding a spiritual community. Listen to your inner voice and pay attention to your circumstances; follow leads to communities near your home or those that are attended by others you know. God will lead you to the right support as you remain in dialogue with prayer.

Spiritual Signs and Messages

Spiritual signs or messages from our children are common but very individual. Signs are subtle messages from the spiritual world that are intended for someone specific. Most people are afraid to admit to experiencing such signs except with a trusted person. One mom asked her daughter a few days following her funeral, "Are you still here?" Immediately her porch gong struck three times on its own. Another mom had a faith statement answered with a vase falling off a shelf—twice. I often have butterflies cross my path or fly into my face, especially when I'm crying or at my daughter's grave site. One mom had a hummingbird tap at her window, and another had a cardinal who banged into the window pane every day. Signs often have signature themes, such as dragonflies, rainbows, pennies, heart-shaped stones, or specific birds or flowers, but they can also be anything and from anyone. Usually they are ordinary circumstances that may come at special times, like a car's license plate passing you with your child's name. The signal to you is both spiritual and physical. Something inside of you tells you that "this is a spiritual sign."

Living in a science-driven society, we tend to discount spiritual cues or events for fear of being accused as "irrational" or "hysterical." Science only entails the physical or empirical world: phenomena that can be measured. The spiritual dimension lies outside the realm of science by its very definition, but that does not mean a spiritual presence does not exist. To those of us who have experienced almost countless signs, they are as real as the food we eat and the air we breathe. Scientific research on such experiences has confirmed the benefit of such spiritual connections for parents (Klass, 1997; Somani & August, 1997; Thompson et al., 2011).

Sometimes moms will receive a certain type of visitation. They may actually see their children very briefly or encounter them in strikingly vivid dreams. Usually, parents only confess to such an occurrence with the most trusted of confidants. Moms may fear "going crazy" or having hallucinations, but these encounters are real, not fantasy. Please know that such experiences are both common and normal (Klass, 1997; Somani & August, 1997).

Signs are meant to comfort us! They are signals that our children are still with us in another way—still living but in a different entity. Often moms get messages that their children are "OK." Sometimes catching a quick glimpse of a deceased loved one can be comforting, but other times it can plunge the person into terrible heartache agony. Either way, the intention of the visit is to comfort and console. Many people speak of "feeling the presence" of a deceased loved one, especially in the months following the funeral. Moms seem to be able to maintain that spiritual contact over the course of many years. One mom hears her son's voice talking to her all the time: not hearing with her ears but with her spiritual-perception skills. I received so many signs of comfort during my most painful grieving periods that I began to expect them. Some moms perceive these signs as comfort from God, others as comfort from their children, and still others from any combination of the two. The most important things to consider are that you should not discount any signs that are given to you and do not question your sanity.

MESSAGES FOR MOMS: SPIRITUAL SIGNS

- ဢ Pay attention to any circumstances that seem to be sending you a signal. Avoid overlooking or discounting coincidental events. If it occurs to you that some event might be a sign, then it probably is. Listen to your inner voice.

- ဢ Share experiences with other spiritual people. Members of the clergy are often familiar with spiritual signs. People who have lost precious loved ones—especially a spouse or a child—may also share their own stories with others who will understand.

- ဢ Take comfort in the signs that are sent to you. They are your connection with your child, who is still ongoing. I keep a journal just of these signs so that I can later look back over the years and remember all the ways that I have been comforted and feel grateful.

- ဢ Talk to your child and ask him or her for signs. They may not come as you expect, but often our interactions can invite spiritual signs. Parents commonly talk to their children for the rest of their lives, which studies have linked to healthy outcomes of bereavement (Arnold & Gemma, 2008; Riches & Dawson, 1998; Thompson et al., 2011).

Finding Hope

There is no justification for your loss. No enormous amount of good, no fund-raising for worthy causes, no huge amount of spiritual growth can justify the catastrophic loss of your child. Your child may be in a "better place," but that does not negate your pain or in any way diminish the extent of your suffering. It is never "OK" that your child is gone from this earth. Regardless of whatever good may come of it, the loss of your child is an unspeakable tragedy and an inconceivable violation of all that we call good.

Despite the tragedy of catastrophic loss and the violation of life with an untimely death, doing some good deed for another person will help heal you. We may not be able to quiet our own pain, but doing something for someone else somehow distracts us and eases our pain. When we cannot restore our lives back to wholeness, giving to someone else is the next best thing. Some moms plunge themselves into volunteer work. Others simply write thank-you notes or bake cookies for those who have been kind to them. In my first year of grief, I would periodically leave flowers on the steps of a family who had just lost their wife and mother. I would do so anonymously so that they would not feel in any way compelled to respond. I gained a small sense of satisfaction in helping someone else who was in pain like mine.

In such giving lies the healing. Some moms help people through their employment; others gravitate to different kinds of ministries or charities. Many simply find themselves becoming more sensitive neighbors or friends than they were before their loss. As your energy slowly comes back and your balance begins to gain strength, you may find yourself leaning toward such work. Follow whatever calls to you in the future. We get back by helping others—sometimes far more than we can understand (Klass, 1997; Harper et al., 2014; Miers, Abbott & Springer, 2012; Rossetto, 2014).

Over time, look for creative outlets and positive aspects that are left in your life. When we grow to realize our loss, honor our lost children, and love those around us, an amazing thing happens to our hearts: they grow bigger. We may not be conscious of any change or aware of any difference in how we interact, yet our caring for others expands and our compassion multiplies. We are able to respond to people who are in pain with deeper empathy and understanding than we could before; we can say words that are helpful in new and meaningful ways. This personal growth will happen on its own and will be a part of your family's journey as well as your own. The one redeeming consolation of watching my surviving child suffer the loss of a sibling was the knowledge that she would be a vastly more compassionate adult because of this hardship, and one who would probably be more equipped to encounter hardship in the future. So will I.

MESSAGES FOR MOMS: FINDING HOPE

- ⍵ As you feel able, find ways to help others, even in small ways, like sending a positive card or e-mail.

- ⍵ Focus on what you still have in your life for which you are grateful.

- ⍵ When you feel ready, look for ways to give to others: follow your heart on a path that feels comfortable and satisfying for you.

CHAPTER 5

Dodging Negative Messages

WELL-INTENTIONED FRIENDS AND family will likely feed you their beliefs, which may be very destructive to you. If you are aware of the messages to ignore, you will be better equipped to let those words bounce off you and then stop the conversation. You may find yourself thinking these beliefs and hearing words from close family members in your child's past come to your mind. I recommend pushing any unhelpful thoughts from your consciousness. Here are a few common messages that many mothers find unhelpful.

The "Closure" Myth

The need for "closure" is another unhelpful common theme, both of conventional religions and of general society. Your faith community may actually mistakenly think that you should reach a point when you will be done with grieving. Mothers never stop missing their children. Moms adjust in healthier ways when they continue to remember and honor their children in rituals and objects, share memories and photos, and connect with their children as spiritual beings for the rest of their lives. Rather than "letting go" and "moving on," research has found that mothers do best when they are encouraged to hold on to memories and connections with their children, thus forming a continuing bond (Arnold & Gemma, 2008; Harper et al., 2011; Klass, 1997; Riches & Dawson, 1998; Thompson et al., 2011).

MESSAGES FOR MOMS: DISARMING "CLOSURE"

- ∞ Incorporate your child's memory into your life without apology and continue to honor him or her in your own way.

- ∞ Educate others that maternal loss is different, and that only other bereaved parents can truly understand. Try to forgive others for any ignorance or unhelpful comments.

- ∞ Remember that research in maternal loss indicates that being spiritually and emotionally connected with your child will result in more positive outcomes over time (Riches & Dawson, 1998; Wijngaards-de Meij et al., 2005). You are the expert on what will be helpful to you.

Judgmental Religion

Even within the same religion or religious community, different people will emphasize different aspects of a belief system. Some religious people focus on the judgmental aspects and take a negative perspective of faith beliefs. The loss of our children is not a punishment to either us or them! If that were true, think of all the criminals who would be dead. Our children's loss is an unspeakable and unexplainable tragedy that has no moral indications for us or for them, regardless of the circumstances. God is all-forgiving to everyone, as most religions prescribe. We do not earn God's forgiveness but rather accept it. Our children have that forgiveness now, and we must trust in that.

MESSAGES FOR MOMS: REJECTING JUDGMENT

ଓ **Look for faithful people and communities who reflect a loving and forgiving God rather than a punishing God. Avoid religious people who espouse views that emphasize a vengeful God, even if they are within your own faith community.**

ଓ **We all make mistakes, but that does not keep us from entering heaven. Seek members of a belief community (or individuals within your community) who emphasize forgiveness and the assurance of eternal life or other views that are helpful to you.**

Denying the Intensity of Loss

Many religious people will try to hide or repress the sadness of loss with the belief that our children are "in a better place." Such expressions are simply using religion to mask the inability of the speaker to confront the full intensity of your pain. True as heaven may be, our suffering is real, our loss catastrophic, and our pain all-too unrelenting. Many moms feel guilty for the extent of their heartache, thinking their sadness means that they are somehow lacking in faith. How tragic for a mother to be further tortured by such a distortion of religious belief. No one needs false guilt added to the agony of losing a child! *Feelings* have no moral value. There is no right and wrong to emotions. Our emotions are the most precious part of who we are. Only actions have moral value or implications. Our grief is an expression of our immense love and dedication that is separate from our faith. The good outcomes of our faith are our hope in the afterlife, our hope in some future good in our lives, and our gratitude for what we have now, but none of these will diminish the pain of loss.

When mothers are made to feel guilty about their grief, they then become forced to hide it. Shame is added to the burden of their pain. Isolation sets in as the bereaved become more reluctant to seek support. I have seen people of deep faith express their grief in inappropriate ways or be hindered from moving into more healthy situations because they have denied their grief. Pain must be processed in order to be relieved. Hindering the expression of such normal feelings will thwart the healing process (Harper et al., 2014). Instead, our faith provides a God who eagerly waits to hear our cries and share our heartache. For Christian mothers, remember that being the Son of God did not make the crucifix any less painful for Jesus, and being a Christian does not make the loss of a child any less painful for us. Our faith offers us invaluable hope and peace in the *midst* of such pain, not anesthesia from it.

MESSAGES FOR MOMS: IGNORING DENIAL

    ଓ **Seek support from other believers or members of the clergy who are emotionally and spiritually equipped to acknowledge the full extent of your pain and offer** spiritual help in healing, such as with prayer. Other bereaved parents may offer recommendations for the right spiritual supportive person.

ఴ Be open to all means of support for your feelings. The help we need often comes from unexpected sources—but often at the time we most need it.

Faith Healing

A fourth common theme in some religious communities is the belief in divine healing as a faith statement. Some individuals think that God heals everyone who has enough faith. These folks imply that my daughter was not healed because we did not pray in some specific way or believe strongly enough in the power of God. Although I am convinced of God's love and care for both me and my children, I reject the notion that humans can control divine action, even by prayer. God heals whom He chooses to heal and allows suffering for a reason, which I cannot understand in this life. I avoid people who may be judgmental or condemning, even if they do practice the same religion as me.

Messages for Moms: Healthy Healing

ఴ Carefully examine the messages you receive and reject those which are destructive to your healing.

ఴ Avoid people who seem to hold viewpoints that reflect judgment of your feelings or actions, punishment for you or your child, or denial of your normal grieving process.

ఆ Seek positive spiritual support to help you move through whatever questions plague you. You may find hospice clergy or grief counselors to be more helpful than your home clergy.

ఆ Seek out support from other moms who have lost a child. The only people who really understand are those who have experienced the same loss.

CHAPTER 6

Hurtful Responses

Fix-It Friends

PEOPLE FEEL HELPLESS in the face of your inconsolable loss. They have an intense need to say something to lessen your pain. They cannot understand that this pain refuses any comfort and must be processed over time to ease. They try to help by saying things that will negate your pain, such as "He's in a better place" or "You can have another child." They may also tell you they know how you feel and compare your loss to their loss of a grandparent, which just feels insulting to you. They may tell you that you "should" not be feeling these deep grief feelings or, worse yet, blame you or your child for your loss (Klass, 1997; Riches & Dawson, 1998). These people are acting out of their own needs to distance themselves from your loss. They are incapable of helping you.

What you need is someone to validate your pain and affirm your own way of handling it. Most people are afraid that if they acknowledge your justified sorrow, you will crumble. They try the "fix-it" approach. Many mothers suffer the unhelpful advice of friends and family to "move on." The cultural taboo of grief in our society just fuels these misconceptions about loss and your needs at this time.

MESSAGES FOR MOMS: AVOIDING FIX-IT FRIENDS

- ☙ **Ignore any indications that you should stop missing or remembering your child, and try to forgive those who make such suggestions. Others cannot begin to appreciate your world or experiences.**

- ☙ **Distance yourself from unhelpful people, especially anyone who has a negative impact on your self-image or your child's memory. Some people are toxic. Avoid them.**

- ☙ **Educate friends and family that everyone heals differently, and you are the best expert on what you need at this time.**

- ☙ **Say your memories out loud! People will avoid the subject of your child for fear of upsetting you until they hear *you* talk about your child first. By sharing your happy memories of your child, you are teaching others that talking about your son or daughter is a welcomed topic.**

- ☙ **Consider giving friends and extended family part 2 of this book. People really want to be helpful, but most just don't know where to start. Let this book inform them.**

ল Remember, you are not in this world to live up to
others' expectations.

Clueless Family Members

Bereaved moms commonly express disappointment in the
lack of support and empathy from family members (Hunt &
Greeff, 2011-2012; Klass, 1997). Often the most hurtful comments come from a mother's family members who simply
cannot understand, including siblings, in-laws, or parents.
We expect more from people who are close to us, so their
inability to respond is all the more devastating to us. Try to
remember that they are frightened, both by the intensity of
your pain and by the terrorizing thought that it could happen to them. Their fear drives them away or renders them
unhelpful.

MESSAGES FOR MOMS: UNHELPFUL FAMILY

ল Try to forgive all those who make insensitive and
hurtful remarks, for the stabs are unintentional.
Hanging on to your resentment just adds more stress
to your life. Remember that they are frightened and
simply limited in their ability to help and respond.

ল Try to let go of expectations. Try to expect nothing of others; just be grateful for whatever they
can give. Your acceptance of their inadequacy to
be helpful preserves relationships and lowers your
frustration.

   Look for support elsewhere. Be grateful for the support that comes from unexpected places: a common experience among bereaved moms.

Needy Grievers

Everyone wants to help, and in the first few months you may be overwhelmed with people coming at you from every side. Those who provide dinners and flowers and hugs are wonderful, although those who bring their grief to you may be more of a drain than a help. People may express their feelings of shock or sorrow or grief to you, which may make you feel the need to comfort them or help them process their own grief. When others put you in the position of supporting them in *their* sorrow, you become the giver. During the first year or two following the loss of a child, most mothers have precious little energy to give!

People who bring their grief to you clearly have no awareness of their actions or the effect of those actions on you. In my case, for example, around the first anniversary, a couple who knew my daughter expressed their eagerness to have dinner with us. The evening was their recounting of all that they had done for my daughter, with never a word of praise or affection for who *she* was. Afterward, I realized that they were grieving the loss of my daughter and using my husband and me as sounding boards to process their own loss. I walked away somewhat traumatized by the lack of affirmation, not only for us but for my precious child. Although they clearly had a great deal of affection for my daughter, they were so wrapped up in their own feelings that they couldn't begin to think about how their words affected us.

We are not obligated to help others process their grief. We can set boundaries for others, though. When my elderly mother would lament the loss of my daughter on the phone, I couldn't bear it. How could I give sympathy to someone else, even my mom, for her loss of *my* child? I simply told my mom to call her pastor, her friends, or my sister. Let others turn to *their* resources, rather than bringing their grief to you. You have all the pain you can handle on your own.

Often, I would not realize that I had overextended myself until after the fact. We are so used to functioning at a certain level that it's difficult to realize the extent of the damage to our minds and bodies. I could easily get so caught up in helping others deal with *their* loss of *my* daughter that I failed to realize how much I had compromised my own well-being in the process.

MESSAGES FOR MOMS: AVOIDING THE NEEDY

- ଔ **Keep in mind that you may feel able to handle someone one day but not the next. Try to avoid committing yourself to future events. Stay flexible and allow yourself to do what you feel like as you feel able at the time.**

- ଔ **Set limits on your social engagements and interactions. Avoid people who say unhelpful things until you are ready to cope with them.**

ଔ   Remember that your situation is terrifying to every
      other parent out there. I found childless women the
      most capable of listening to my pain, because they
      were not vulnerable to the same tragedy.

ଔ   Set boundaries on conversations. Explain to others
      what you will discuss and what you will not. Retelling
      the trauma of the details of the loss may destruc-
      tively reinforce all your posttraumatic stress, thus
      resulting in more grief symptoms from the interac-
      tion. You are not obligated to tell anyone anything.

ଔ   Focus on the positive. If people ask questions about
      your child's death that you don't want to discuss,
      rechannel the conversation. Say, "We just want to
      remember what a wonderful man he was and all that
      he did for his family." Use it as an opportunity to
      tell them about how precious your child is and all he
      or she means to you.

The Timid and Frightened

One mother recounted, "I feel like I have a sign around my
neck saying: 'I just lost my child.' People avoid me because they
don't know what to say." People may be relieved that you are
not crying, since they are uncomfortable with your loss or ter-
rified that the same fate may happen to them. After losing a
child, you find out which of your friends have the emotional
fortitude to listen to your pain or even look you in the eyes.
Feeling left out or socially ignored is a common experience for
most bereaved mothers (Thrift & Coyle, 2005).

MESSAGE FOR MOMS: TURNING OFF THE TIMID

   ଔ **You cannot control other people's behavior. Try to forgive them (for your own sake) and actively find people who can support you. As bereaved mothers, we all have friends who are no longer our friends, but we also make new friends who are even better!**

The Judges

People will evaluate how well you are coping, which can be infuriating. If you carry on normally, they will wonder what is wrong with you or assume you are in denial. If you cry all the time, they will judge you as not coping well and will tell you to see a therapist. There's no winning at this game: you have to ignore all evaluations except those of extremely trusted friends or counselors or, best of all, another mom who has suffered loss. No one else understands.

MESSAGES FOR MOMS: IGNORING JUDGES

   ଔ **The only way to protect yourself from judgmental comments or unhelpful suggestions is to hide your pain from those who cannot understand. Share your grief only with those who can be supportive: usually others who have experienced loss of some kind.**

   ଔ **Give yourself permission to limit your social contacts and to find new supports in other bereaved parents. See the resource list at the end of this book for more information.**

ଔ Try writing down comments that anger you and then burning the paper as a safe way of venting the rage and letting it go. You need to try to forgive others for not knowing how to help, both for your sake and theirs.

ଔ Consider seeking counseling so that you can have a safe sounding board for your pain and your anger. Friends get tired of listening to people's grief. Bereaved-parent support groups or grief counselors provide a specific opportunity to process these intense feelings without adding demands to your social relationships.

ଔ Be selective so that you can find a counselor who appreciates parents' extended periods of anguish, which are normally more intense and prolonged than with other forms of relationship loss. Keep in mind that any diagnostic labels are only for third-party billing purposes for the clinician. There is nothing pathological or complicated about intense grief extending for years for bereaved parents, but the health-care system in the United States has no well-supported services to meet these expected needs.

CHAPTER 7

Your Identity

Who Am I Now?

SOMETIMES THE LOSS of our child changes our own identity: Are we still a mother to our child? How do we now respond to the question, "How many children do you have?" That question alone points to our difficult position.

Mothers will answer this question in many different ways, all of which are acceptable. You might respond with, "I have one surviving child," thereby indicating that you've experienced a loss. Many parents respond with the total number of their children and are prepared to explain where these children are now. Some bereaved parents respond with, "That's a loaded question" or "That's a sad story." Such introductory statements pave the way to explaining your circumstances. Some parents feel strongly that they should always acknowledge all their children. Other parents need to protect themselves from probing questions from strangers that will lead to uncomfortable conversations, and, therefore, speak of only their surviving children. There are no right or wrong answers to these questions. You may change how you respond depending on the situation, what you are feeling at the moment, and where you are in your healing journey.

MESSAGES FOR MOMS: WHO AM I

- ℘ Always listen to your inner voice and respond in ways that feel comfortable.

- ℘ You will always be your child's mother. No one can ever take that relationship from you.

- ℘ Continue your relationship with your son in his spiritual form. Talk to your daughter; feel her presence as you are able. You are still your child's mother, and your child is still there for you, but in a different form.

- ℘ Be open to other ways to be a mother and other lives to touch. Your deep sorrow enlarges your heart and opens your capacity to help others over time. Caring for others in any way or form is another way of continuing your child's memory as well as your own mothering skills. Many mothers have been transformed by the continuation of their mothering to others who are in need; in this way they also serve as an extension of their children's lives (Farnsworth & Allen, 1996).

Impact on Self-Esteem

The pain of grief feels awful. The emptiness and aching of loss renders us virtually nonfunctional and covered with sorrow. We unconsciously feel unworthy of love and attention when we are in so much pain. We cannot feel good about ourselves when our world is so black. Yet, studies have indicated that bereaved parents who were able to hang on to their feelings of self-worth had less depression and fewer traumatic-stress symptoms (Engelkemeyer & Marwit, 2008; Mancini et al., 2011).

We all need as much specific positive feedback as we can get, but even more so in the months following catastrophic loss. Seek out those people who can reinforce you. It's OK to let your close family and friends know that you are feeling awful about yourself or even to ask them for affirmation.

One mom told me, "If one more person tells me I'm doing so well, I'm going to smack them!" Nonspecific feedback is not helpful, especially when we feel completely demolished. Often when people tell you how great you are coping, they really mean, "Thank God you are not an emotional mess, because I wouldn't be able to handle it!"

What we need is recognition for all the specific tasks we are doing well, such as maintaining social contact appropriately, making daily decisions, and caring for ourselves and our families. In the first and second year following catastrophic loss, such everyday activities now take great courage, energy, and inner strength. We need others to reflect back to us what we *are* doing well as well as the good things they see in us. Even the smallest acknowledgement is helpful, such as the way we write a thank-you note or our ability to smile. Unfortunately, few people are able to provide such detailed compliments.

Messages for Moms: Self-Esteem

- ❧ Let those closest to you know that you are vulnerable and need more positive reinforcement than you normally would. Share part 2 of this book, which offers specific direction.

- ❧ Build your own self-concept in positive ways. Write down what you did each day, giving yourself a star for every little thing—like getting out of bed!

- ❧ Say one positive word to each family member, and know that you have just given them a huge gift.

- ❧ Savor whatever good comments come to you, capturing them in a journal or posting them on your wall.

- ❧ You are a hero. You survived the first few days and months of catastrophic loss. Give yourself credit for breathing. Each day takes courage.

CHAPTER 8

Helping Your Children and Spouse

Your Surviving Children

WATCHING OUR CHILDREN grieve compounds our own heartache. Your surviving children may be the most sensitive to your own grief and will try to protect you from their pain. Depending on the age of your children, they may be frightened by your tears and sorrows or irrationally blame themselves for the loss of their brother/sister. They will have the same feelings of regret for things they've said and done in the past and may feel tremendous guilt for still being alive. They may feel inadequate in ever being as good as their lost sibling, fearing they will never be able to make you as happy as you were with their sibling. Most of all, they are catapulted into the same dysfunctional state of shock, inability to concentrate, and consuming preoccupation with the lost sibling in addition to having physical symptoms such as insomnia and fatigue. They may be unaware of all the complexities of their emotions and likely will be unable to verbalize or express them. Yet, our culture expects these poor children to carry on as normal! They are expected to perform in work or school as if nothing has happened, as if their entire world has not come crashing down around them.

Living in our Western culture that denies or ignores grief adds to our children's torture. I have been amazed at educators' lack of understanding and insight into the rhythms of grief, the length of the grieving process, and the needs of children. Unfortunately, you will need to advocate for your surviving children in the months and years to come.

MESSAGES FOR MOMS: SURVIVING CHILDREN

ᘓ Give your surviving children tons of affection and positive reinforcement. Grief makes us all feel badly about ourselves. You are the most powerful person to counter the negative impact of loss on your children. Even though you are racked with pain yourself and can barely move, you need to give as much specific positive feedback and loving concern to each of your surviving children as you can possibly muster. Other than caring for yourself, this is the most important work you can do following loss.

ᘓ Lower your expectations for a year or two. Your surviving children will be irritable and grumpy or may fly into rages and tantrums without warning. They will have no energy for work or school. They will not be able to concentrate and perform as usual. They will likely regress temporarily in their developmental stage or engage in rebellious, acting-out behavior as an expression of their pain and anger at their loss. Such disturbing behaviors will decrease as your children slowly heal. In order for them to process this loss, they need time and space. Crowded schedules packed with activity and full of demands will only impede their healing. Getting your children through the next year able to function and not slip into depression is more important than grades, acquired skills, or career preparation or success.

ଓ Help them lower their self-expectations: reassure them that they have years ahead of them when they will be able to perform optimally in order to catch up on anything they're missing now. Explain that their lack of concentration while grieving is a result of their love for their sibling. Just as a broken leg limits your functioning for a while, healing takes time and rest. Reassure them that they are growing a bigger heart in the process and that this is perhaps even more important growth than they will experience in their academics. Truly, they will become more compassionate adults from surviving this tragedy. For adult children, teach them the realities of grief: this loss will affect them for much longer than they would like. Advise them to construct their work life with realistic goals for the near future. Encourage them to find positive support as well as accurate information about the length and normal experiences of the grieving process. Many bereaved-parent groups also welcome young-adult siblings.

ଓ Advocate for your children. Run interference with the school system, coaches, or any other potential sources of pressure. I made contact with my child's advisor each year; I explained our loss and how it had affected my child. The birthday and anniversary of my lost daughter were particularly dysfunctional days each year for her sister. I needed to explain this to her teachers and insist on a few allowances for extra time to get her work done.

ভ Set up support for your children. Mothers commonly express concern about their ability to care for their family members during times of intense grief (Elder & Burke, 2015). Certainly, you will be limited by your pain. Accept your limitations and try to solicit help from close friends and family members—or any other source you can find. Your surviving children need to be able to openly share their feelings with someone other than family members. They may find such support on their own. One middle-school boy would ask to be excused from classes and go to his guidance counselor to talk whenever he felt overwhelmed with grief. Another high school student sought out the school nurse, who offered a comforting ear and supporting presence. In addition to such resources at school, evaluate whether or not counseling might help your child. You might approach your children by explaining that this is *your need* to help them. Explain that you need to make sure that their needs to talk and be understood are getting met, rather than them thinking that something is "wrong" with them. Hospices often have grief counselors or resources they can recommend. A few communities have agencies for children in grief or summer camp programs. Explore all options and try to encourage your children to attend if you think one of these options might help. Although agencies for grieving children are relatively hard to find, contacting the social-work department of a children's hospital or unit may give you a few leads to follow; parental-bereavement groups may also have information on children's resources for your local area.

cs Provide other outlets for your children's expression of pain. Many children and teens find physical activity to be a helpful outlet. Buy a punching bag, trampoline, or a family membership to the YMCA. Provide art materials for creative expressions. One middle-school girl found soothing comfort in a simple painting-by-numbers kit. Keep in mind that activities that may seem mindless actually allow your children to process loss at a different level. Give credit to their instincts and allow them to choose their own means of expression (within healthy boundaries).

Husbands and Partners

The catastrophic loss of a child imposes enormous stress on a marriage. Your bond with your spouse will either grow incredibly stronger or be dissolved, depending on how you handle your grief and treat each other. This section speaks to four important aspects of maintaining a strong bond: grief expression, timing, mood changes, and physical intimacy.

Grieving differences. Men grieve differently than women do. Studies of bereaved parents have found that the intensity and expression of grief both vary among men and women. Mothers tend to be more expressive in crying and talking, while fathers often use busyness or tasks as an outlet for their pain. (Alam, Barrera, D'Agostino & Nicholas, 2012; Avelin, Radestad, Saflud, Wredling & Erlandsson, 2013; Hunt & Greeff, 2011-2012; Talbot, 1997).

Both parents feel as if they have just been run over by a truck. Both feel devastated, dysfunctional, racked with pain, and crushed to the core. Some people react by suppressing the pain as much as possible and by "moving on," which can be infuriating to the other parent, who copes with the same loss through uncontrollable crying. There is no "right" way to grieve. Whatever your instincts are telling you is likely the best thing for you to do—which may be entirely different from your spouse's behavior.

Problems may potentially happen when parents have different grieving styles. We tend to unconsciously judge ourselves as not grieving "well" because we are grieving differently. When racked with the agony of loss, holding on to your self-worth so that you can grieve in your own way is very difficult for both partners. The stoic parent may feel guilty for not being more demonstrative, while the wailing parent may feel pathetic for not being "stronger." If both parents feel defensive about their coping styles, communication may break down, which can trigger a negative cycle. Guilt associated with the loss for either partner affects the other partner, thus compounding the grief (Barr, 2012). Research has shown that couples who avoid talking to each other about their loss experience more grief reactions than those who are able to share openly both their emotions and their continued bonds with their lost children (Bergstraesser, Inglin, Hornung & Landolt, 2015; Stroebe et al., 2013).

Although parents often try to protect each other from more pain by not discussing their suffering, such avoidance often produces the opposite result. Giving each other respect, attention, and an acceptance of differences helps maintain the relationship and enhances your ability to integrate the memory of your child into your marriage (Bergstraesser et al., 2015). Counseling intervention may be a helpful option to allow both parents to feel validated in their individual ways of coping, understanding differences, and accepting and hearing each other's expressions.

A husband will sometimes be fearful of the intensity of his wife's grieving and of the length of time that will be involved. I've heard of one husband reassuring another husband that his wife would someday stop crying but that it might "take a few years." Husbands fear that they will never see their wives laugh or enjoy life again, just as we fear the same for ourselves. But we will heal. It just takes so much longer than we want it to!

MESSAGE FOR MOMS: GRIEVING DIFFERENCES

   ଔ **Ask your husband to give you time, and reassure him that everyone tells you it gets better but that it usually takes a year or two.**

Timing differences. The timing of grieving varies greatly for each individual. Grief comes in waves, interspersed with a few brighter spots. When you finally get your head above the waterline to think of something other than your loss for a few minutes, you may not want your spouse to pull you back into your grief at that moment. Yet, your spouse may be in the middle of a huge wave of grief and may need someone he can share his loss with, or vice versa. The impact of the loss will hit each person at different times. You may feel angry that your husband can be cheery when you are racked with pain, or you may feel irritated that he has brought you back to your grief in the few minutes you were able to think about something else. All these dynamics are normal and common and will further stress the relationship.

MESSAGES FOR MOMS: TIMING DIFFERENCES

ભ **Accepting each other's differences and lowering our expectations of each other are both critical to maintaining positive spousal relationships. We automatically look to our husbands to be our "grief partners." Sometimes they can take on that role, while at other times they will not be able to do so. Accept and love them at whichever stage they are at the moment, for their loss is as great as yours—just expressed and processed differently than yours.**

ભ **Get support from multiple sources beyond your husband: one person cannot carry all your emotional needs. The more people supporting you, the better your needs will be met. Parent-bereavement groups and professional counselors offer you another set** of ears, thus easing your pain and isolation. Seeking such support is not a sign of weakness but rather a creative use of resources.

Irritability and anger. Often the excruciating loss of a child elicits our anger. The normal human reaction is to take that anger out on the people closest to us: those who "should" understand. In grieving families, everyone is feeling the same intense pain. Families who are grieving typically bicker and fight, which means they displace their anger on one another. Rather than releasing the pain, such arguments simply compound the awful feelings we have about ourselves. We desperately long for affection and connection but end up pushing away those people we need the most, who themselves are incapacitated by pain.

MESSAGES FOR MOMS: IRRITABILITY

○ȝ **Ignore the negative. Try hard to forgive yourself and your husband and children. Forgive them for being irritable and exhausted. Forgive them for expecting too much of you and for not giving enough. Forgive them for being self-absorbed and inconsiderate. Try to forgive them for whatever they are doing that angers you, for they are also in intense emotional pain. When they lash out at you with sharp words, try to respond with patience rather than more anger. Ignore the negative and give back positive. Leave the situation until you can regain your composure, let go of your anger, and see your husband as a partner in experiencing this** excruciating pain of loss. As difficult as such patience may be, your calm response will be critical to preserving the relationship in the long term.

cs Acknowledge your limitations. When a harsh remark escapes your lips, apologize as soon as you possibly can and explain, "I'm just irritable because I miss our child." By connecting your own negativity to your grieving process, you are acting as a role model for your family so that they can see how to be in touch with their feelings. You are showing them how to repair damage done from harsh words. Even though you may be irritable, this has nothing to do with your loved ones actual worth or your love for them. When you slip and take your anger out on your family, you need to correct that mistake as soon as possible by making it clear that the problem is not them. Your own loss is the really distressing factor that makes every other minor irritation unbearable. It is never too late to apologize and repair damage to a relationship with loving words and hugs.

cs Reflect back the positive. Look for ways to build up and reinforce your husband and children. Make a point of trying to find one positive thing they do each day that you can thank them for, even if it's a chore they've been doing automatically for years, such as taking out the garbage or making their beds in the morning. Each effort will now take more energy. Acknowledge the littlest things they do. You will be amazed at what a few kind words can do to heal their hearts. Seeing them smile or brighten up—even for a moment—from your loving words will be helpful to you as well.

ᘓ **Find emotional support.** You need to have people outside your family to listen to your pain and reinforce your worth. Friends, extended family members, other bereaved parents, members of the clergy, and counselors are all sources of help and support. If arguments continue to escalate, seek professional help as soon as possible. Often couples simply need to understand how loss profoundly affects them to get through the first year or two intact.

Affliction often bonds people closer together. The loss of a child often either drives couples apart or strengthens their marriage in amazing ways. How we handle the loss and treat each other makes all the difference in the survival of the marriage and family.

Physical intimacy. Parents commonly stop sexual activity immediately after the loss of a child. One study found that over half resumed intimacy by three months after the loss, albeit with reduced frequency. The mothers in the study often felt that any such pleasure was "wrong" after such a tragedy, more so than was the case with the men who were studied. The men in the study commonly perceived their wives' need for physical comfort as a need for sex rather than just a need for affection and closeness (Dyregrov & Gjestad, 2011). As in all aspects of grief survival, this is highly individual; each couple will experience unique needs.

MESSAGE FOR MOMS: PHYSICAL INTIMACY

ଓ **Talk to your spouse about your feelings and needs. Remember that grief does soften over time and that your life will return to more "normal" patterns eventually, even though life will never be the same again. Your child would want your marriage to survive and for your bond with each other to remain close.**

Single Moms

Single bereaved moms have added challenges and often less social support than married moms, which may augment the pain of grief (Barrera et al., 2007). You may long for a partner who misses your child as much as you do. You may feel more isolated and more overwhelmed with caring for your surviving children and for yourself. Taking time off from work to grieve may not be an option for you. Clearly, you have specific stressors in your life from your full-time parenting role that add another difficult dimension to your grief.

MESSAGES FOR MOMS: SINGLE MOM SUPPORT

ଓ **Get help in every way possible. This is no time to try to be a hero or prove that you are a superwoman. You need to rally every possible source of support. Doing so is not an acknowledgment of weakness; instead, it** is a smart move to strengthen your position and provide for yourself and your surviving children.

ଔ Investigate your health insurance for mental-health coverage, and seek professional counseling. Your therapist can serve as the "other" voice you need; in this way, your therapist can help you work out your parenting concerns for your surviving children and can act as a sounding board for your grief. Think of this as hiring a best friend, and use this strategy as much as possible.

ଔ If at all possible for you, try to let your counselor and friends/family know that you need positive feedback. You need them to reflect back everything they see that you are doing well; this feedback will be critical fuel for your mental health. Send them part 2 of this book (written for those who wish to support a bereaved mother), which clearly describes these needs.

ଔ Look for community resources:
- grief support from hospice or local health-care places
- community social work departments for referrals or information
- school counselors for your surviving children's needs
- church or civic groups that may provide assistance with meals or diversion activities for your children

CꙄ Accept every offer of physical and practical help that comes to you. Let your friends/family know when you need their support both emotionally and physically. No one will understand how long the fatigue and sadness of grief lasts, so we must educate them. You will need to continue to solicit help as the months go by.

CꙄ Look for groups for bereaved parents in your area, and try to contact some of these people. Ask for advice for resources and possible special groups for single mothers. A list of such organizations may be found in the back of this book.

CꙄ Keep a gratitude journal. Focus on the positive in your life as much as possible. Keeping mindful of any comfort in your life is a powerful mental-health tool (Sin & Lyubomirsky, 2009).

CHAPTER 9

Honoring Your Child

THERE ARE TWO parts to grieving: expressing the pain of loss and honoring the one who has been lost. Honoring our children can be as simple as placing a picture on a table or as involved as engaging in fund-raising activities. There are a great many and varied ways to honor our children, and many opportunities to do so will come and evolve over time. Below are a few thoughts and examples.

Multiple studies have documented the very real need for parents to continue the bond with their children for the rest of their lives. Many parents have reported linking objects or symbolic representations of their children, such as butterflies or cardinals, into their daily lives. Tending the grave is another way of honoring them and connecting with them. Many bereaved parents recommend continuing the bond, and perceive greater healing when they do so (Arnold & Gemma, 2008; Harper et al., 2011; Klass, 1997; Thompson et al., 2011; Tan, Docherty, Barfield & Brandon, 2012).

Each family is different. Some people do activities as a family, while other activities involve only one family member. Some activities would be therapeutic for some family members but horrifically painful for others. An open house for your child's friends or a special church service may be just what you crave but would be too much for your surviving children or even your husband to handle. While fund-raising for a scholarship or charity may overwhelm you, this could be the perfect activity for your husband to focus his grief in a positive direction. Let each of them do what is healing for them at their chosen time, without forced participation by others. Give yourself permission to do what is good for you, even if your husband and children are uncomfortable participating. We all heal differently in our own way and time. Your surviving children may do their honoring decades from now, and this is perfectly fine. There are no rules and no time limits to healing. If necessary, find friends or extended family members who may join you in your honoring activities.

The suggestions below are simply meant to stimulate thoughts about some activities that may comfort you. What matters is not the project itself but the comfort the activity brings to you. Sometimes, we cannot know what will help until we try something. The goal is surviving this loss; you will learn as you move through your grief.

A few possible ways of honoring include

- ♥ **creating photo albums or photo books for yourself or others;**
- ♥ **writing down memories in a journal as they come to you;**
- ♥ **inserting captions or narrative comments to photos albums;**

- ♥ making a quilt of your child's T-shirts (or hiring someone to do it for you);
- ♥ displaying important mementos in frames or tables;
- ♥ duplicating your child's creations (one mom reproduced the gift baskets that her daughter had made the previous year);
- ♥ leaving flowers or notes on the grave site;
- ♥ painting rocks as love notes in your garden or on your child's grave;
- ♥ reproducing your child's writing or artwork for friends and family;
- ♥ creating a scrapbook of the letters and cards you've received that tell about your child's precious strengths and talents;
- ♥ creating a website (or having one created) that honors your child and invites comments;
- ♥ planting a bush, tree, or garden;
- ♥ starting an annual tradition (one family decorates a tree in the yard on their child's birthday in the child's memory);
- ♥ writing a love note on a balloon and releasing it into the sky.

As time goes on, you and your family may decide to tackle a bigger project. Some families start scholarship funds in their child's memory, provide funds for an award in the child's name, or create their own philanthropies. Some become valuable resources or educators to work against the circumstances that contributed to their child's loss. Others raise funds for a room, garden, or other space to be named for their child. Some families hold fund-raising events each year for charities that were special to their child or have special meaning. Honoring your child in a way that also helps others means that you are coping with the pain of loss in a positive way, one that has helped to ease the pain for many other bereaved parents (Rossetto, 2014).

There are as many different ways to honor as there are imaginations to conceive of them. You can do different things on different years, or you can invite others to join you or just privately remember alone. Find the ways to continue your child's memory that best fit the needs of you and your family at this time, and be flexible in the years to come.

CHAPTER 10

Coping over Time: Changes in Grief

GRIEF CHANGES OVER time, but it doesn't change nearly as quickly as we would like. Often, our pain gets worse before it gets better. The months following the initial shock may feel even harder as the first year unfolds. Sometimes the reality of the loss hits people with a new blunt awareness during the second half of the year: my child really is not coming back. As time goes on, the full impact of the loss can strike you with new force: the loss can sink even deeper into your soul and consciousness and contribute to your struggle to heal.

Just as your grief becomes more real, the rest of the people in your world may begin to treat you as they normally do. "Helper fatigue" has set in with your extended family and friends, who are now over *their* shock and are now back to focusing on their own lives. The helpful casseroles, notes, or phone calls drop off, which leaves you with the impression that you are *supposed* to feel better—but you don't. The pain is as real as ever, if not worse, and the waves of grief are coming as frequently and fiercely as ever. You have healed enough to allow more of the pain to seep up into your consciousness. Although you have made progress, you may be unable to detect any healing just yet.

MESSAGES FOR MOMS: COPING OVER TIME

ଔ All the things you did for yourself the first few months are the healing things you need to continue. Allow yourself as much time and space as you need to grieve, cry, mourn, and rest.

ଔ Grief symptoms usually cluster: when you are feeling sad, for example, you may also experience more fatigue, insomnia, or inability to concentrate. Often the physical and cognitive symptoms of my grief signaled to me that I was reacting to triggers in my environment. Fighting these symptoms or getting frustrated with yourself will not help. Your body and mind are healing in their own way and in their own time. Do whatever seems helpful for you at this time. Crying and acknowledging the pain once more may be the only way to ease these symptoms.

ଔ Remember that your family is also experiencing ongoing pain, even though everyone has returned to his or her "normal" routine. Your husband and children may protect you from their grief. Each of the suggestions for supporting your family members will apply for the next two or three years, at least. Catastrophic loss requires slow and gradual healing over a long period of time.

ଔ Look for support wherever you can find it. You may be feeling well enough to contact another mom who has lost a child, for example. Check the organizations listed at the end of this book for local chapters in your area.

ଓ Lower your expectations of yourself. We all expect to be "all better" in a few months, which is an unrealistic expectation following catastrophic loss. We need more time to rest, more time to remember, and more time to just be still than we did before. You may look back at the past couple of months and wonder how you managed to do what you just did, but now is the time to cut back as much as possible. Give yourself time during your days and weeks to honor your child in your thoughts, and take time for naps or rest periods. Bereavement is exhausting.

ଓ Turn off your self-critical voice and focus on what you are doing. Every action is difficult, and any action means you are making progress, from doing laundry to driving your children to school. Walking into a room of people and smiling takes tremendous courage following a loss. Giving a hug to your children or husband means that you are expending energy in important ways. Give yourself a pat on the back for every positive action you do.

ଓ Remember that you will heal, but it will take several years. Many peer counselors see mothers move from living in unspeakable, dysfunctional distress to creating meaningful, satisfying lives and learning to trust the process that will slowly unfold over time. "Two steps forward, one step back" will eventually move you to healing. I have seen amazing transformations of the lives of bereaved mothers. The thunderstorms do eventually ease, and you *will* see the sun again.

CHAPTER 11

The First Anniversary

THE BLACK DAY that marks a year since the loss of your child is simply called "the anniversary"; some call this day their child's "angel date." Unlike other dates on the calendar, this day holds a huge weight in our lives. I was surprised at the impact of the first anniversary on my body and mind, even though I had been forewarned. I felt the clouds of grief growing darker again six weeks in advance. I experienced a resurgence of grief symptoms: physical, cognitive, and emotional. Even before I started worrying about how this date would feel, my body had unconsciously begun to anticipate this dark reminder of my extreme loss.

Our family decided to hold an anniversary church service, even though doing so was not our church's tradition. Our minister was extremely supportive, and we elicited help from a small group of friends. Putting together the event was painful, because we were focusing on our loss, which triggered more pain. I chose to do this because it was another opportunity to publicly honor my daughter, which was important to me. I also knew that each of my daughter's college friends would be remembering that day and the shock of hearing about her death. They would want to be together, and I wanted to be with them.

My surviving child could not handle the thought of another memorial service, so we allowed her to stay at home. My daughter's boyfriend, now involved in another relationship, was also absent. The empty chairs next to me were sad, of course, but I chose to accept everyone's differences in grieving. We gave everyone who knew our daughter permission to heal in their own ways, forgiveness when they could not join us in grieving in our way, and unconditional love regardless of their actions.

"What will people think?" became a familiar refrain in my mind. Would folks in our church think that by holding a service, we were "not coping well"? Would our friends think we were "bad parents" at not insisting that our surviving child be there? I chose to ignore this negative thinking and simply did what my heart told me was the right thing to do. We cannot control the thoughts or judgment of others. If you find that you are beginning to wonder what people think, try to dismiss the thought from your mind. We cannot control the thoughts of others, and those thoughts do not matter. What matters is that you remain true to your own healing process.

We had a simple service with a PowerPoint presentation of my daughter. My pastor spoke and invited people to share stories and memories about Melissa. I treasured every word, and when we got home I wrote down everything I could remember. We had a simple reception at the church following the service. People lingered for over an hour, and we heard more wonderful stories about our daughter. I came home deeply grateful for that evening and extremely glad that I had done this service.

When anticipating the first anniversary, I appreciate the horror that some parents will feel at the thought of putting themselves through anything resembling a memorial service. Other parents experience similar anxiety prior to a first-time fund-raising or any other public event in their child's honor. The initial impact of our loss is so completely devastating that we fear doing anything that might even remotely rekindle the same devastating reaction. Those same fearful parents expressed gratitude *after* these events, however. The event itself was usually not as difficult as they had feared, while the ability to honor their child was just as satisfying to them as it was for me. Just seeing their child's name in print again eased their pain. You may need to wait a year or more before you can do anything on the anniversary. Give yourself permission to change and heal differently as time passes.

MESSAGES FOR MOMS: THE ANNIVERSARY

- As appropriate, be open and direct about your needs; let people know how to help you remember your child or get through the weeks before and after the anniversary.

- None of your friends and family can understand what you are experiencing, and everyone heals differently. It doesn't matter what others think: the only expert on your healing is you.

- Give other family members freedom to decline any involvement, or negotiate a compromise with them.

MESSAGES FOR MOMS: HONORING THE DAY
BELOW ARE A FEW POSSIBLE SUGGESTIONS FOR THIS DAY.

- ℅ Perhaps provide a structured gathering in a more formal way to share memories, light a candle, or say a prayer. I have had Melissa's friends gather to paint small rocks with love notes for her grave site or for their gardens. Others have provided helium balloons for love notes to release into the sky all at the same time. Those who knew your child will also be remembering and grieving, so think about including them in an honoring activity.

- ℅ Consider creating a remembrance of your child; some moms find this helpful to ease the pain of the first anniversary. A simple pamphlet or booklet with photos, drawings, or writings to give or mail to others marks the day in a different way and furthers your child's memory.

- ℅ One mother I've heard of asks others to write her child's name somewhere and send her a photo. I used this idea for one anniversary and received dozens of photos of my daughter's name creatively displayed in many ways from various places. The challenge of creativity added to the fun for others while bringing the memory of my child to their minds. One of Melissa's friends reported feeling incredible satisfaction spelling Melissa's name out in Legos with her own young children. Such positive, creative activities help others to express their sorrow in meaningful ways, as well as helping you.

ଔ Perhaps create a PowerPoint presentation to post on a website or present to a small group of close family members.

ଔ Some families prefer more intimate marking of the day. The list in chapter 4 offers more ideas for ways to honor your child.

ଔ *Choose whatever will best comfort your heart.* There are many ways to mark this day, and all are correct, acceptable, and wise.

CHAPTER 12

Second-Year Losses

Unrealistic Expectations

OVER TIME, YOUR support from family and friends will dwindle. Some of their concern and attention will fall off after the first few months or following the first anniversary. People have healed from their trauma of your loss and are simply going on with their lives; they've forgotten the intensity of your pain.

Few of us can sustain intense caring for another person over long periods of time. Even more disturbing: friends and family may assume that you are "over it." They may actually think that you have healed from your loss and have "moved on," or, worse yet, they may think you should have if you haven't! People who have not experienced catastrophic loss are usually incapable of understanding.

I felt embarrassed by my grief. My close friends would want to know how I was in general, but I was afraid to mention what really plagued my mind. Old grief is old news. People tire of hearing about it, and feel helpless to respond. Our friends unconsciously dismiss our pain by their neglect of our feelings, their ignorance, and their continuing with their own happy, intact families. We feel more lonely and isolated by the contrast, perhaps even with our closest friends.

Three months following my first anniversary, I returned to my teaching job after having the summer off. Everyone interacted with me as if I were the original strong, towering World Trade Center. In reality, I was the post-9/11 ground zero and still smoldering. It was a bizarre contrast that added even more of a burden to the weight of grief I was already experiencing. Those who have experienced catastrophic loss find that it takes a long, long time to fully regain their former functioning status. Many moms say that it takes three years to adjust to the loss, as reported in several studies (Arnold & Gemma, 2009; Feigelman et al., 2009; Klass, 1997).

Even though our lives are never the same, we do regain functioning eventually, but it does not happen nearly as quickly as we would like. Some people report the second year feeling almost as difficult as the first year. Although I doubt others noticed a difference in my functioning at the time, I knew I was not capable of the same productivity the second year after loss in compared to my functioning in earlier years. The stress of grief was a constant companion that demanded some of my attention and energy, which was appropriate and right for me to do at that time. Although I sufficiently fulfilled my work obligations, I also had to cut myself a little slack as needed and set realistic goals, given the added emotional demands on my psyche, even in the second year. It doesn't matter if anyone understands. It only matters that you listen to your body's cue and take good care of yourself!

MESSAGES FOR MOMS: MANAGING EXPECTATIONS

03 **Educate those who are close to you or those who seem open and compassionate. Let them know that your**

grieving will not parallel their loss of an elderly parent or grandparent. Your healing is more long term.

ॐ Give them positive ways to help you; these will also help them. The second part of this book is for you to give to others who wish to support you.

ॐ When close friends and family members no longer seem capable of sustaining support and understanding, try to forgive them.

ॐ For support, reach out to other moms who have experienced loss. Moms who are further down the road of healing can offer you comfort, reinforcement, and hope.

ॐ Perhaps consider helping a mother who has very recently lost a child or some other person in need. I found that supporting moms who had more recent losses than mine was very therapeutic for me. I saw by contrast how far I had progressed in my own healing. If you have not yet joined a bereaved-parent support group, now might be a good time for your own healing.

Secondary Losses

In addition to losing your child, you have lost all the normal daily activities or contacts with people whom your child brought into your life. You may no longer be chatting with the other soccer moms, for example, or seeing friends at the playgroup or PTA meetings. You may no longer be going to college football games or having the familiar sounds of sleepovers. You may have lost contact with your adult child's friends who used to frequent your home, or you may now have much less contact with your grandchildren. The losses that accompany your child's loss are equally real, and they legitimately add to your pain.

MESSAGES FOR MOMS: SECONDARY LOSSES

- ❧ **Acknowledge these losses and grieve for them along with the loss of your child. Sometimes just feeling the loss and expressing it is the best we can do.**

- ❧ **Look for other ways to connect to people who were important to you or to your child. I routinely send occasion cards to my daughter's young-adult friends as a way of staying connected, and I periodically invite them to our house. The contact with others who loved my daughter is invaluable, but it does require some effort. Depending on what's happening in their lives, some of these friends come in and out of our lives, which is as it should be. I consider each contact a gift and, since I am expecting nothing, I am deeply grateful for whatever comes.**

- ❧ **Form new bonds. The only people who will really understand what you are experiencing are other mothers who have experienced loss.**

Unfinished Business

With a little bit of time—a year or two past the loss—you may be able to assess what negative feelings are still haunting you and then work at letting them go. You may still feel guilty about circumstances or events surrounding the event, for example. Now may be the time to try to let go of some of these negative feelings. Forgiving yourself is a huge gift that is necessary for your healing.

Each person's journey to self-forgiveness and forgiving others will be different. My faith teaches me that God forgives everything—if we accept that forgiveness. If God forgives me, than who am I to continue to blame myself? Sometimes I first need to ask forgiveness of someone else in order to forgive myself. I've simply asked my daughter to forgive me whenever regrets come to mind. Other people have written letters or notes to their lost loved ones in which they ask for their forgiveness. Often I need help forgiving myself or others, and I pray for that help. If I decide to focus on forgiving and pray whenever I feel guilty or angry, I find that these negative feelings do subside over time. Whatever your worldview, the first step in healing is deciding to let go of guilt or anger.

Some parents have additional stressors surrounding the type of death. When criminal or legal proceedings are involved, for example, excruciatingly painful work is dragged out for years. Your healing is impaired by the continual reminder that more work has to be done: more testimonies, more lawyers, more focus on the most tragic and painful part of your loss. Not only do these reminders continue to pour acid into your emotional wounds, but the repeated and prolonged steps perpetuate all your worst nightmares and re-etch the negative memories deeper in your mind. All of this results in unavoidable additional trauma. No wonder you are angry! As justified and unavoidable as your rage may be, such fury will eat away your mental and physical health. Your anger will result in more harm to you and those you love than to the person (or people) who deserve it.

Forgiveness is another aspect of letting go of anger. Forgiveness is *not* excusing or forgetting wrongdoing or failure to punish. Justice can still be done with forgiveness. Forgiveness is simply letting go of anger and hatred: seeing the other person as broken, ill, or spiritually and morally crippled and choosing to let go of your hostility. They are still responsible for their actions and need to suffer the consequences, but you choose to let go of your resentment. Letting go of anger is likely to be a long, repeated, and painful process, but doing so will reap great benefits to your mental, emotional, and physical health in the long run as well as in your relationships with others (Hunt & Greeff, 2011-2012). Many bereaved parents have reported finding key support in spiritual communities or other faith resources (Thompson et al., 2011). One study of bereaved parents found that healing from grief was more strongly related to having a sense of purpose in life than the cause of the child's death (Rogers, Floyd, Seltzer, Greenberg & Hong, 2008). While we never truly "get over" the loss of our children, we do heal in such a way that we can build meaningful lives while working toward positive goals.

"Tsunami" Days

As time progresses, you may find that you cry a little less, laugh a little more, see sunshine a bit brighter. Then you have a "tsunami" day: the intensity of your loss suddenly hits you like a fifty-foot wave and drags you helplessly under its power. The grief is so overwhelming that you just want to cry all day. Since we tend to think we have passed beyond such passionate expressions of sorrow, such feelings can be both alarming and painful. Most parents occasionally have these kinds of strong grieving episodes—even during the second and third years—and find that they generally only last a day or two.

MESSAGES FOR MOMS: SURVIVING TSUNAMI DAYS

- ❧ **Don't be frightened by tsunami days, which are normal and to be expected. They will become less frequent and less intense in the years to come and will eventually disappear.**

- ❧ **Lower your expectations of yourself on tough days. Give yourself a break.**

- ❧ **Find some way to express your grief; trying to push the pain underground will not relieve it. As tough as it sounds, embrace the pain of loss by engaging in remembrance activities. Visit the grave site, light a candle, look through photos, write in a journal, or choose some other way to remember your child.**

- ❧ **Be open to whatever may help: a massage, a prayer, a walk, a nap, reading scripture, doing a jigsaw puzzle, drinking a cup of soothing tea, or reading the comics. The list is endless and individual.**

ଔ Call a friend. Look for support among those who can understand and support you in positive ways—especially other mothers who have experienced loss.

ଔ Know that tomorrow will be better. Tsunami days usually only last one day, and sometimes only a few hours. After giving ourselves a chance to mourn, we will emerge more capable of turning our attention to something else.

CHAPTER 13

❧

The Third Year and Beyond

IF YOU HAVE not yet experienced the first anniversary of your loss, please do not read this chapter until at least twenty months following your loss. Get through the initial period before thinking about coping in the long term. You want to take healing one day and one step at a time.

For those of you who have made it through the first twenty months or so of your loss, below are several common long-term themes for bereaved mothers that should be helpful to you.

A Constant Companion

If you are entering your third year, you now know that this pain does not dissipate quickly. But you have also successfully survived the first two years! You have negotiated the holidays, endured the insensitive remarks, ignored the hints that you should be grieving differently, and found ways to heal. You have become an expert in your own healing, which is huge.

At some point, most mothers slowly come to realize that their grief will always be a part of their lives, even though it does ease over time. Normalcy creeps back into our lives. We slowly move our energy to a more balanced swing between loss and living positively. Our days are more sun than rain and continue to grow brighter with each year, although never without an occasional storm of grief (Arnold & Gemma, 2008; Hunt & Greeff, 2011-2012; Klass, 1997; Wijngaards-de Meij et al., 2005).

If your friends and family expected you to be healed after the first year, they will *really* expect you to be done grieving by now. You have probably been holding back on sharing your true level of grief for two years now, since you are aware of how quickly people will tire of hearing about your loss.

MESSAGES FOR MOMS: CONTINUED GRIEF

- ⍵ Look back at your survival, and give yourself enormous credit for your progress through the most difficult part.

- ⍵ Forgive those who used to be your most reliable supports who may now have forgotten about your grief. Be thankful for the positive role they played in the past, and look for new support.

- ⍵ Continue to engage in all the grieving activities that have comforted you so far, including crying, writing, and talking to "safe" people.

- ⍵ If you have not yet made contact with other mothers who have lost a child, consider doing so now. For some mothers, these relationships will be more valuable when their grief is less acute.

ଓ Ignore any suggestions that you "should" be past your mourning, for people who make such suggestions misunderstand the distinction and uniqueness of the loss of a child.

The Lost Future

Over time, we begin to miss not only the child we had but the person who would have been with us now. We wonder how their lives would have progressed, what they would have done. As we see their contemporaries moving through the normal stages of life and the usual milestones—graduations, weddings, and births—we become painfully aware of the absence of our lost child. We miss not only the child we knew but also the young adult or older adult we never got to know.

MESSAGES FOR MOMS: LOST FUTURE

ଓ Like all grief-related pain, accept this loss. Know that these feelings are normal, and embrace them.

ଓ Try to create a new future by using different kinds of meaningful engagement. Look for ways to invest in the next generation that will comfort you, or give back to others in some way that calls to you.

The Real Future

Mothers commonly fear a future without their children, but they avoid admitting this, sometimes even to themselves. We all hope our children will be our comfort in our old age, even if just emotionally or socially. After all, we have lost a huge part of our anticipated future with the loss of our child's earthly life. We grieve not only our current loss but our future losses! Like all aspects of grief, there is no avoiding this pain. We need to acknowledge this future loss and know that every parent feels some part of this loss, too. We are not "selfish" to hurt from the absence of our children in our futures and the loss of the pleasure of their adult support in the years to come. This is legitimate loss that deserves our tears and time.

MESSAGE FOR MOMS: THE NEW FUTURE

Ë **Just as support came when we needed it these past two years, support will come to us in the future. Engage in helpful communities of adults who care for one another, whether social groups or religious groups. We can create "family" in nontraditional ways.**

Holding Memories

We also fear the fading of memories of our precious child, worrying that current and future events might crowd out the cherished moments of the past. These fears are normal. Some believe that we will not only see our children again in the afterlife but will regain any lost memories at that same moment. Once we are rejoined with our children as spiritual beings, we will feel as if we had never been separated. Time will stand still when we enter eternity.

MESSAGES FOR MOMS: MEMORIES

- ℭ **Write down your memories or capture your thoughts by audio as you go through your child's possessions or photos. Having your memories secure will ease your mind.**

- ℭ **Give yourself permission to form new memories, new bonds, new experiences, and to laugh and sing again! Your love for your child can be expressed in savoring every day of living, smiling at the happy memories. and loving those around you now. Living positively in hope and humor will continue to honor your child in a different way than your tears do.**

Staying Connected

As the years progress into the third or fourth year, you will gradually feel more able to really engage in life. Some moms feel guilty for not grieving as intensely as before, even while they are relieved to be able to focus on something else for a time. Such regret is normal, but being in somewhat less pain in no way indicates that we have less love. We gradually grow accustomed to having our child as a spiritual rather than physical presence. We heal enough to function more completely. Our precious children are always in our hearts and minds but without overpowering all other thoughts.

MESSAGES FOR MOMS: STAYING CONNECTED

- ℭ **Continue to talk to your child and incorporate him or her into your daily activities. In this way, you bring your child into your future with you.**

115

ఴ Continue to engage in any and all honoring activities for your child as you need or desire. There is never a time when we have to stop remembering privately or publicly.

ఴ Know that you are honoring your child in your heart even as you regain a healthy balance in your life and start to engage in every moment to the fullest.

Transformation

For a bereaved mother, grief never ends (Hunt & Greeff, 2011-2012). We always miss our children's earthly presence. We always carry them in our heart. We always long to talk to them. Our yearning for our child gradually becomes one theme among several in our lives rather than our predominant tune. Over many years, our honoring moves from distressing mourning to a cherishing and treasuring of their lives. Our grief becomes mixed with gratitude for every minute and memory as we move from agonizing lamentation of the loss to a combination of sadness and bittersweet celebration of the life and gift of this child. Our continued honoring, talking, and remembering are all forms of celebrating this precious life and staying connected with our children.

At some point, many mothers look back and realize that they have grown through all the trauma and loss. Their hearts did indeed enlarge. Their compassion is more encompassing, their self-knowledge more in-depth. Such personal growth in no way justifies our tragic loss, but it does equip us to better help others—to allow some redemption to spring from the devastation of loss. As you use your compassion to help others, so do you continue to celebrate the life of your child (Cacciatore et al., 2013-2014; Engelkemeyer & Marwit, 2008; Lichtenthal, Currier, Neimeyer & Keesee, 2010; Rogers et al., 2008; Somanti & August, 1997).

May you find meaning in your journey, companionship along the road, and peace in your life.

Part 2: How to Help the Bereaved Mother

Specific Actions to Support a Grieving Mom for
Friends, Family, and Everyone Else Who Cares

Beyond the Imagination

Losing a child is like having both your legs blown off by a land mine. Even if you see the land mine and brace yourself for the impact, the destructive explosion still blows you to pieces. If someone had explained to me the emotional, cognitive, and physical damage that was wrought by losing a child, I would not have believed the degree of destruction to these otherwise healthy, well-adjusted women. I could only comprehend the extent of the damage by experiencing it myself.

At first the grief is accompanied by numbness: a fog that surrounds a mother, even in the midst of excruciating pain. Somehow she continues to function, to act normally, and even to make decisions. After a few months, the reality sets into her brain with new horrifying confrontation: her child will not magically reappear as she unconsciously halfway expected. The disbelief has given way to an even deeper grief, just as all her friends and most family members have recovered from their shock and have gone on with their lives in the assumption that she is now better.

You do not need to appreciate the level of destruction to this mother to be extremely helpful, but you do need to avoid making judgments about how well she is coping. She will protect herself from such judgmental eyes and will allow herself to be vulnerable only to those with true compassion and courage to feel the pain with her. The following are practical guidelines on how best to be supportive of a mother who has lost a child.

Grief has no age limits. This lost daughter remains a child to her mother regardless of how old she may be. A mother does not see the loss as any less tragic for a sixty-year-old son than for a stillborn infant. Her grief spans all the years that her child was on earth, mourning every memory. For a successful child/adult, she will grieve the loss of his or her fruitful years ahead. For a disabled or troubled child, she will mourn the loss of an opportunity for that child to find healing and wholeness. For a stillborn, she will mourn the loss of her child's future. There is no characteristic of the child that makes the loss less catastrophic or devastating for the mother. In this book, the term "child" refers to a mother's offspring at any age from birth to older adult.

Pitfalls to Avoid

Know thyself. Before you do or say anything, come to terms with your own limitations, and admit them to yourself. You may desperately want to help, but if you have children of your own, this situation may simply terrify you. This mom needs support from others who can listen and affirm her. If you feel paralyzed by your own fears, you can use the ways of helping listed below that will be doable for you. Share your positive thoughts and appreciation for this child in a note or letter. Such appreciation for a loved one who has been lost will be enormously helpful to all grieving families.

Avoid thinking that you can fix this pain. Please do not be fooled into thinking that the mother will ever be all better or that she will heal according to a time plan that seems reasonable to anyone else. Her catastrophic loss of her child parallels a disabling assault. Since her trauma is invisible, we fail to understand the level of devastation. Compare the loss of a child to a physical trauma. First she is in the intensive care unit for months before moving on to the step-down unit. Since grief comes in waves that recycle and return, she will periodically move back and forth between being dissolved by grief and being relatively functional. She will hide her more vulnerable moments from those who cannot understand or judge her behavior. The first anniversary may put her back in the ICU for a month before and after the event, as will major holidays or family milestones. Eventually—maybe in the second or third year following the loss—she will move to rehabilitation, with only occasional bouts of complications that may put her back into hospitalization. You may never see this fluctuation, because within the first year, she may be walking without a noticeable limp. But it takes huge effort and pain for her to walk so smoothly: this is effort and pain she dare not admit to, for no one understands and everyone judges. After three to five years, she probably has healed as much as she can; she has resumed her life and has found new ways to heal and express her grief in positive ways. She can walk without too much pain or effort. You see her as being all better, all healed, just like an amputee who has completely adjusted to the loss of limbs. In reality, every night she looks at her missing legs and never stops wishing she could dance again. A mother misses her son and longs for him, yearns for him, every day for the rest of her life. While you cannot change her need for her child, simply *acknowledging* such yearning will be hugely helpful and therapeutic to her.

Avoid trying to cheer the mother up by changing subjects or distracting her. My dear friends wanted desperately for me to be happy on my birthday, which just made me feel even worse. No one can distract a grieving mother from her deceased child; any attempts to do so simply force the mother to push her feelings underground, thus increasing her sense of isolation and loneliness (Hunt & Greeff, 2011-2012; Klass, 1997; Lehman, Ellard & Wortman, 1986). Instead, ask her what *she* wants most to do and then be willing to engage in an activity that honors her child, even if it makes you sad. One mom requested company while she spent time at her child's grave site. Bereaved mothers need friends who can be with them in the remembering instead of being forced to pretend to be "fine."

Avoid focusing on the positive aspects of the child's loss, such as with the comfort that "she is in a better place." No matter how wonderful heaven may be, the mother remains racked with pain at the loss of ever again seeing, hearing, touching, and having her child. This mother needs friends and family who can feel the pain with her and validate her grief. Comments that minimize the loss add insult to her injury, which negates the legitimacy of her mourning and makes her feel that it is socially unacceptable to be sad.

Avoid assigning meaning to the loss. Any explanation for why this tragedy happened will likely infuriate the mother (Breen & O'Connor, 2011; Lehman et al., 1986). Only she can find the meaning in this pain for herself. Just listen to her feelings, whatever they may be, and know that her views will likely change over time.

Avoid identifying with the mother's feelings, such as by saying "I know how you feel." Bereaved parents often report feeling offended by such comments (Lehman et al., 1986). The mother does not need you to know or understand; she wants you to listen and accept her own experience.

Avoid thinking that anyone else can fix this pain. There are no magic bullets. Telling a mother that she needs therapy because she is crying shows rejection of her bereavement and disapproval of her coping skills. Such negative feedback will make her angry and will indicate that you are not a safe or supportive person. She may benefit from something such as a sleeping medication in the immediate days following loss, and suggesting that she should seek medical advice for such topics is fine as long as you include the reassurance that insomnia is normal in bereavement. Mothers may benefit from having a nonjudgmental professional person to talk to, or they may benefit from wise counsel about handling the bereavement issues of other family members. Recommendations for professional help should be made simply to offer supplemental support and guidance in the healing process, and not to offer "closure." *Please* understand that no one can take away this pain, and medication will dull the pain but will not heal her. Only time can heal this wound, and she will never stop missing her child. The most therapeutic response you can offer is reassurance that her emotional response is normal, all grief is individual, and that there is no set end point. Try to separate her need to take years to process this loss from your need to see her "better." This is *her* loss. Do what is best for her.

Lower your expectations of this mother. Dismiss all conceptions you might have about timelines for healing or what she "should" be doing. Grief work is hugely individual. Rather, encourage her to trust whatever her inner voice is telling her to do. Remember, she is forever changed. Imposing some arbitrary timeline for healing is destructive to bereaved parents (Hunt & Greeff, 2011-2012).

Avoid giving advice. Everyone heals differently. Only the mother can identify the best path for her to take now. Allow the mother to choose what to do with her child's possessions or photos, for instance. Many bereaved parents continue to keep their child's room in their house for as long as they are able to do so. Commonly, bereaved mothers need to stay home for a while or just rest for months. Avoid all judgments, for only another bereaved parent can truly understand. If the mother is meeting her own physical care needs and making functional decisions, then she is coping well, regardless of how destroyed she may seem. Extreme sorrow and crying are appropriate reactions; these are signs of coping in bereavement. Studies have shown that bereaved parents have repeatedly identified advice from friends as being unhelpful (Barrera et al., 2009; Hunt & Greeff, 2011-2012; Lehman et al., 1986).

Avoid encouraging them to find "closure." Parents will long for their children for the rest of their lives, often intensely. Although the grief will soften over several years, this will not occur until three to five years following the loss (Arnold & Gemma, 2008; Feigelman et al., 2009; Klass, 1997).

In the case of a violent death, the easing of pain and the subsiding of posttraumatic symptoms may take many years (Kristensen, Dyregrov, Dyregrov & Heir, 2016; Murphy, Johnson & Lohan, 2002). Although friends and family long to see the mother less grief-stricken, burying the pain of loss is often associated with greater grief symptoms over time (Harper et al., 2014).

Avoid suggesting that the mother should be "moving on" or somehow experiencing less pain, since this will anger bereaved parents. Bereaved parents do *not* experience the theoretical "grief stages" but rather a mixture of intense emotions swirling and waving that gradually ease over the years. The grief of losing a child is lifelong for bereaved parents; they find meaning, fulfillment, and healing in honoring their children in many continual ways. Encourage their memories and join them in memorials and remembrances (Arnold & Gemma, 2008; Breen & O'Connor, 2011; Dean, McClement, Bone, Daeninck & Nelson, 2005; Klass, 1997; Lehman et al., 1986).

Avoid generalized positive comments such as "You look so good" or "You are doing so well!" Such comments usually mean, "Thank God you are not an emotional mess, because I would not know what to say to you!" If the mother seems to be coping extremely well and interacting normally in the months or even years following her loss, she has simply learned to hide her pain. Refer to the section below on providing *specific* positive reinforcement, since this is critically important.

Encourage her tears. If your conversation leads to tears, you have successfully created a safe environment where this mom can be honest and release her pain. Tears are a compliment to your relationship. Just touch her in whatever way is comfortable for both of you and continue to listen. Assure her that her tears are releasing the pain and making room for healing. Tears are necessary and healthy. Hugs are often the best response.

Key Support: Praise for Her Child

Say positive things about the lost child. Mothers *hunger* for words of affirmation about their children. They hang on to these comments like lifelines and treasure them in their hearts. A grieving mother never stops wanting to hear the positive characteristics of her child and all that made her child precious. She longs to know that others saw her child as being special and all that made her son or daughter so (Barrera et al., 2009; Breen & O'Connor, 2011; Lehman et al., 1986; Oliver, Sturlevant, Scheetz & Fallat, 2001; Woodgate, 2006).

I can name the women who wrote these kinds of *specific* positive things about my daughter in a note after our loss. I put these notes in a special place. You need to take time and thought to *describe exactly* all the ways that this child was special or accomplished. General comments like "wonderful man" or "great kid" are helpful but not powerful. Potent descriptions include "he always had a kind word for others," "she had a smile that brightened up a room," "he knew how to read his teammates and gave encouragement to guys just when they needed it," "she had irresistible and charismatic personality and charm," or "he showed great leadership by…" Although describing such traits specifically can be challenging, it is the most therapeutic gift you can give! Multiple studies on loss have found that bereaved adults long to hear positive messages about their lost loved ones and that these messages may improve their own functioning (Bonanno, Mihalecz & LeJeune, 1999; Kunkel & Dennis, 2003; Rack, Burleson, Bodie, Holmstrom & Servaty-Seib, 2008).

Recount a positive memory! If you can think of a specific event, however small, that showed the child's personality, *please* write it down for this family. It can be as minor as "I remember how everyone would look up when she entered a room, because she was so gorgeous," or "He made friends with everyone at school," or "Someone needed a crayon, and he was the first to offer it—so typical of his goodness." Of course, more lengthy stories are even better, but even short, specific memories are more precious than gold to this family! You will most likely recall them in the weeks following the child's death, so write them down when you do, even if just in a note to yourself. As time goes on, these memories will become even more precious to this mother. It will never be too late to share them—even years later.

Listen to the mother tell you about her child. If you are capable of allowing the mother to recount her memories, listening to her will be a huge, priceless gift. People mistakenly believe that bringing up the child's name or memory will be painful to the mother, as if she can possibly forget her son or daughter! Giving her an opportunity to tell those memories that surround her mind and fill her life will provide the best support possible, as research has shown (Arnold & Gemma, 2008; Toller, 2005).

Since most people avoid the topic, mothers learn to avoid mentioning their children, which just adds to their pain. One of the most profound moments of support I received in the past six years came when one of Melissa's friends asked me to tell her about a memory that I had just mentioned in passing. You can simply say, "What do you miss most about your child?" or "Can you share a memory with me?" or "Do you have any photos you can show me?" If you indicate that you truly want to sit and listen, you will quickly elicit memories from this mother. Simply respond to her with reinforcement for the special attributes of her child and you will be giving her the best support possible. Please remember that listening is itself a gift of help for this mother.

If the mother wishes, send any photos you may have of the child and make copies to send again in future years. When you lose a child, you are never again able to take another photo. Every remembrance becomes monumental; for some mothers this happens right away, while for others it might not be until years later. Some mothers find photos to be too painful in the first year or two. Other mothers will be hungry for photos but less capable of keeping track of anything when they are in such deep distress. Send photos when the mother indicates that she would welcome them. Consider offering the photos again much later; this renews the memories all over again and allows her to do something more organized with the photos now that the crisis of immediate loss has past.

Studies have shown that bereaved parents need to stay connected to their children for life, and they experience lower grief symptoms when they do so (Harper et al., 2011; Norton & Francesca, 2014; Thompson et al., 2011).

Include the child in family events or milestone celebrations. Bereaved parents report deep pain and anger when their lost child is ignored in future family events, as if that child had not existed (Hunt & Greeff, 2011-2012; Klass, 1997). Include a photo, a reading, or a symbol of the child chosen by the parent. Including the lost child in all family celebrations comforts the parents in huge ways, showing your understanding and support of their feelings and loss. As long as the parent is alive, they will want their child acknowledged in some way. Give them this precious gift.

Provide Emotional Support

Reach out, listen to, and affirm the mother's grief experience and reaction as normal and expected, no matter how devastated she may be! Although it will make you feel helpless to "just listen," giving her an empathic ear and positive feedback are exactly what she most desperately needs. Studies show that bereaved parents often try to teach friends how to acknowledge their pain and share their loss (Arnold & Gemma, 2008; Klass, 1997).

Friends often avoid bereaved parents, which increases their pain through isolation. Initiating contact and listening will provide huge comfort to a bereaved mother, who will be consumed by grief and will desperately need to share what she is experiencing with someone. Bereaved parents most need your hugs and your caring presence, as many studies have reported (Barrera et al., 2009; Breen & O'Connor, 2011; Dean et al., 2005; Dyregrov, 2005-2006; Hunt & Greeff, 2011-2012; Lehman et al., 1986; McBride & Toller, 2011; Oliver et al., 2001; Titus & de Souza, 2011; Toller, 2005).

Provide positive reinforcement. Every decision is difficult, every movement painful. Point out every tiny thing she is currently doing, and reinforce all the positive ways she is communicating and coping. Do this as often as you possibly can! Specific, positive reinforcement is the *best* healing medicine in any loss or crisis. In some cases, you may be able to see a change in her mood as you provide *specific* positive reinforcement. For example: "I admire your ability to smile" or "It takes courage to walk into a room of people following a loss" or "You show such strength to continue with your work even when you are obviously in such deep grief." Concentrate on identifying all the mother's innate and acquired strengths, and provide detailed descriptions of those strengths back to her. Focus her attention on her small accomplishments each day, for every task is a major milestone during grief healing. Reinforce everything you appreciate about her. Even a sincere compliment on her appearance or home decor will be helpful. Positive feedback about specific behaviors and accomplishments provides invaluable nourishment and much-needed help for her self-esteem, which automatically plummets in grief. Research has shown that mothers who can hang on to their sense of self-worth are more likely to experience emotional growth and healing (Engelkemeyer & Marwit, 2008).

Help the mother lower her self-expectations. If she is appropriately dressed and sitting up, she is coping well. She will think she can do more than is reasonable following catastrophic loss. Help her to lower her own goals in order to give energy to her bereavement. The fatigue of grief is overwhelming. Encourage her to rest and let go of her own expectations for herself for a while.

Provide physical help. In the first weeks and months following a loss, the mother feels a level of fatigue similar to a bad case of the flu (Hunt & Greeff, 2011-2012). It hurts to move. Mothers also commonly experience other physical signs of stress, including stomach or intestinal distress, back or leg pain, hormonal irregularities, and increased susceptibility to infectious diseases such as colds and flu (Buckley et al., 2012). The fatigue alone is incapacitating and can last over a year! Offer concrete help with meals, shopping, laundry, or whatever you may be able to do. Instead of saying, "Let me know what I can do for you," just do what you can for her. You can also offer concrete help for specific chores: "Can I do your food shopping this week?" or "I'm free Saturday afternoon to help with your errands." Such specific offers sound (and are) genuine. Although the physical toll on the mother is greatest in the first six to twelve months, providing support around the anniversary date or birthday of her child is also extremely thoughtful and helpful (Barrera et al., 2009; Dyregrov, 2005-2006).

Provide empathy. Do say: "My heart goes out to you" or "I'm holding you in my prayers" or "I can't imagine how awful this is for you." Avoid saying, "I'm sorry for your loss," even though this is the most standard response in our culture. Expressing sympathy puts the bereaved in the position of having to return an expression of gratitude. Do use touch to show your support, if that is comfortable for you and comfortable for the bereaved mother. One woman at work just rubbed my back in passing during a meeting, which communicated volumes. It meant the world to me.

Stay calm. Although her level of emotional distress is extreme and her dysfunction frightening, she will heal. We who work with bereaved mothers have seen dramatic transformation from complete devastation to the creation of rewarding lives, but this takes many years! The first *two* years are still the initial recovery period. Many parents report needing at least three to five years to adjust, although they will never feel the same (Arnold & Gemma, 2008; Feigelman et al., 20082009; Klass, 1997). Trust the process of healing slowly, and encourage her to do the same.

Provide Spiritual Support

Reinforce the positive messages of the mother's belief system. Many mothers move on a spiritual journey that may take them into other aspects of faith. If both you and the mother share a faith, you can be hugely helpful in affirming positive messages of forgiveness for her and her child as well as the hope of reunion with her child.

Encourage her to cry to God, rant and rave her anger at God, and be assured of God's love for her no matter what she is feeling. Maintaining a dialogue with God and seeking help from

God hastens the pathway to peace for many people of faith (Arnold & Gemma, 2008; Thompson et al., 2011; Wijngaards-de Meij et al., 2005).

Affirm the legitimacy of her excruciating pain. Remember that her child being present "in a better place" in no way diminishes the pain and suffering of never having that child on earth again! Acknowledging the appropriateness of the grieving represents healing, while negating such normal reactions will further the damage to the mother. No promise of heaven, no matter how real, diminishes the pain of loss to her earthly life. In spite of having very real and deep faith, bereaved mothers experience immense pain. No faith can dull or numb the pain of loss; instead, beliefs can provide strength to cope and have hope in the future.

If she believes that she will see her child again, affirm her belief! The separation is temporary—excruciating, but temporary. Reinforce her hope that she can know she will see her child again and never have to say good-bye. Having a belief in an afterlife has been shown to help bereaved parents (Hunt & Greeff, 2011-2012). If your own belief system precludes you from offering such comfort, please remain silent on the topic.

Respect this mother's right to her own beliefs, and avoid sharing unhelpful views. If she chooses to change her traditional beliefs to meet her needs, respect her choices and her needs. This is not the time for theological debates but for unconditional love from her friends.

Pray with the mother, if she wants to, and definitely pray *for* her, if that fits your worldview. Pray that she will have peace even in the midst of pain.

Encourage the mother to be open to spiritual signs. Mothers often receive spiritual signs from their children. If you are able to appreciate and affirm these signs, you will be helping the mother tremendously.

Provide Long-Term Support

Very few people appreciate the huge gift of long-term support to the mother by continuing to talk about her child and remembering important dates. Usually, only those who loved the child deeply will continue to remember the child's birthday or anniversary, yet a bereaved mother's biggest fear is that her child will be forgotten (Breen & O'Connor, 2011; Dean et al., 2005; Oliver et al., 2001; Toller, 2005). Parents treasure the friends and family who appreciate the critical importance of those days and join the mother in honoring her child and acknowledging the day. I would much rather people remember my daughter's birthday than my own. How priceless it is to hear from others spontaneously that my daughter is in their thoughts, and even better to hear something positive of how they remember her. The longer the time since the loss of her child, the more precious your card or phone call will be to this mother!

No matter how many years go by, a mother will never stop wanting to tell you about her child. No matter how many decades have passed, a mother will always long to hear something positive about her child. If you are one of her remaining friends who remembers her child, you have a very precious gift to offer her, especially on the painful weeks of birthdays and anniversaries. If you never knew her child, you can be equally valuable by asking for her memories and encouraging her to share about her child. Parents long for such opportunities their entire lives, and they hide these needs due to social pressures, yet they heal better with such social support in place (Dyregrov, 2005-2006; Oliver et al., 2001; Thuen, 1997; Toller, 2005).

Below are a few more tips.

- ℭ *Write down on your calendar* the child's death anniversary and birthdates. Don't rely on your memory over time. Insert an alert on your phone or computer.
- ℭ *Send a card or make a phone call,* or both! It's easy to get busy on that day and forget, so sending something ahead of time is great insurance. On the card, just say something positive about the child and acknowledge that this is a sad day for the mother. Acknowledging the pain of that day, even decades later, provides an enormous emotional support. You cannot fix the pain, but acknowledging the pain actually *does* lessen the suffering by providing understanding and acceptance.
- ℭ *Provide time to listen to memories* or look at photos with the mother; this is a huge gift.
- ℭ *Remember that grief spans the week and even the month* of the birthday or anniversary, not just the one day. If you cannot respond on that day, it is *never* too late to call, bring food, or send flowers.

ଔ *Remember that a mother never forgets her child* and never forgets her child's birthday or death anniversary, unless she is suffering from severe dementia. People think they are bringing up painful memories if they mention the child, but the opposite is true. Talking about the child eases the mother's pain of loss and provides comfort to her. You are bringing her the consolation of a piece of memory. Even though her child is no longer here, she can at least talk about him or her with someone. Your presence with her memories relieves the loneliness and isolation of grieving alone, which makes this time with her a precious gift (Dyregrov, 2005-2006; Oliver et al., 2001; Thuen, 1997; Toller, 2005).

ଔ *Mother's Day and family holidays are times to honor her child.* Family gatherings are always reminders of her lost child. Mentioning her child and honoring the child in some way is hugely helpful to bereaved mothers (Klass, 1997).

ଔ *Remember that no expression of support is "too much."* Many mothers report hiding their grief over the years, except to other mothers who have also lost children or a few "safe" friends (Thuen, 1997). Exceptionally sensitive people will bring flowers, food, or time to listen for all the years to come. Any simple acknowledgement of the depth of the loss and the degree of longing for the lost child is hugely therapeutic.

The mother may express guilt or embarrassment when you bring these gifts of time and remembrance. We live in a culture that assumes that grief only lasts a year. I've even encountered many health professionals who have this misunderstanding. We are taught that we "should" not be grieving for years. After receiving negative signals or social cues related to their ongoing mourning, many mothers learn to share their true feelings only with other parents who have also lost a child. Simply let the mother know that you are thinking of her child on this day and that you know she is, too. Your remembrance will mean the world to her in any way that you express it.

Your support increases in value with every passing year. As fewer and fewer people mention her child or acknowledge her child's life and wonderful qualities, those who do will become priceless jewels in the mother's life. Blessings to you for providing her with this invaluable comfort!

Appendix: Resources for Bereaved Parents

Author's note: Below are national groups found throughout the United States, most of which will have local chapters near you. You may also find other local groups in your area that are not listed here. Search the Internet for peer support near you, use online forums, or find a local chapter of one of the groups below.

The Compassionate Friends
http://www.compassionatefriends.org/home.aspx
"The mission of The Compassionate Friends: When a child dies, at any age, the family suffers intense pain and may feel hopeless and isolated. The Compassionate Friends provides highly personal comfort, hope, and support to every family experiencing the death of a son or a daughter, a brother or a sister, or a grandchild, and helps others better assist the grieving family."

Bereaved Parents of America
http://www.bereavedparentsusa.org/index.htm
"The Bereaved Parents of America (BP/USA) is a national nonprofit self-help group that offers support, understanding, compassion, and hope, especially to the newly bereaved, be they bereaved parents, grandparents, or siblings struggling to rebuild their lives after the death of their children, grandchildren, or siblings."

National Organization of Parents of Murdered Children, Inc.

http://www.pomc.org/

"POMC makes the difference through ongoing emotional support, education, prevention, advocacy, and awareness." The POMC vision statement is to "provide support and assistance to all survivors of homicide victims while working to create a world free of murder."

Mothers Against Drunk Drivers (MADD)

http://www.madd.org/

MADD's mission statement is to "aid the victims of crimes performed by individuals driving under the influence of alcohol or drugs, to aid the families of such victims, and to increase public awareness of the problem of drinking and drugged driving."

Tragedy Assistance Program for Survivors (TAPS)

http://www.taps.org/

"TAPS is the 24/7 tragedy assistance resource for ANYONE who has suffered the loss of a military loved one, regardless of the relationship to the deceased or the circumstance of the death."

Healing Hearts for Bereaved Parents

http://www.healingheart.net/

"Healing Hearts for Bereaved Parents is dedicated to providing grief support and services to parents who are suffering as the result of the death of their child or children."

MISS Foundation: Mothers in Sympathy and Support

http://www.misschildren.org/

"The MISS Foundation is an international 501(c)3, volunteer-based organization providing CARE [counseling, advocacy, research, and education] services to families experiencing the death of a child."

Survivors of Suicide

http://www.survivorsofsuicide.com/about.shtml

A website "to help those who have lost a loved one to suicide resolve their grief and pain in their own personal way."

References

Alam, R., Barrera, M., D'Agostino, N. & Nicholas, D. (2012). Bereavement experiences of mothers and fathers over time after the death of a child due to cancer. *Death Studies, 36*, 1–22. doi: 10.1080/07481187.2011.553312

Arnold, J. & Gemma, P. B. (2008). The continuing process of parental grief. *Death Studies,* 22, 658–674. doi: 10.1080/07481180802215718

Avelin, P., Radestad, I., Saflud, K., Wredling, R. & Erlandsson, K. (2013). Parental grief and relationships after the loss of a stillborn baby. *Midwifery, 29*, 668–673. doi.org/10.1016/j.midw.2012.06.007

Barr, P. (2012). Negative self-conscious emotion & grief: an actor-partner analysis in couples bereaved by stillbirth or neonatal death. *Psychology and Psychotherapy: Theory, Research & Practice, 85*, 310–326. doi: 10.1111/j.2044-8341.2011.02034.x

Barr, P. & Cacciatore, J. (2007-2008). Problematic emotions and maternal grief. *Omega: Journal of Death and Dying, 5*(4), 331–348. doi: 10.2190/OM.56.4.b

Barrera, M., D'Agostino, N., Schneiderman, G., Tallett, S., Spencer, L. & Jovcevska, V. (2007). Patterns of parental bereavement following the loss of a child and related factors. *Omega: Journal of Death and Dying,* 55(2), 145–167. doi: 10.2190/OM.55.2.d

Barrera, M., O'Connor, K., D'Agostino, N., Spencer, L., Nicholas, D., Jovcevska, V. & Tallet, S. (2009). Early parental adjustment and bereavement after childhood cancer death. *Death Studies, 33,* 497–520. doi: 10.1080/07481180902961153

Bergstraesser, E., Inglin, S., Hornung, R. & Landolt, M. (2015). Dyadic coping of parents after the death of a child. *Death Studies, 39,* 128–138. doi: 10.1080/07481187.2014.920434

Bohannon, J. R. (1991). Religiosity related to grief levels of bereaved mothers and fathers. *Omega: Journal of Death and Dying, 23,* 153–159.

Bonanno, G. A. & Kaltman, S. (2001). The varieties of grief experience. *Clinical Psychology Review, 21*(5), 705–734.

Bonanno, G. A., Mihalecz, M. C. & LeJeune, J. T (1999). The core emotion themes of conjugal loss. *Motivation and Emotion, 23*(3), 175–201.

Bouckaert, C. M. V. (2000). *Interventions for bereaved mothers: A study of perceived effectiveness.* (Unpublished dissertation abstract: 2000-95018-251.)

Breen, L. J. & O'Connor, M. (2011). Family and social networks after bereavement: experiences of support, change and isolation. *Journal of Family Therapy, 33,* 98–120. doi: 10.1111/j.1467-6427.2010.00495.x

Buckley, T., Sunari, D., Marshall, A., Bartrop, R., McKinley, S. & Tofler, G. (2012). Physiological correlates of bereavement and the impact of bereavement interventions. *Dialogues in Clinical Neuroscience, 14*(2), 129–139.

Cacciatore, J. & Bushfield, S. (2007). Stillbirth: The mother's experience and implications for improving care. *Journal of Social Work in End-of-Life & Palliative Care,* 3(3), 59–79. doi:10.1300/J457v03n03_06

Cacciatore, J., Lacasse, J., Lietz, C. & McPherson, J. (2013-2014). A parent's tears: Primary results from the traumatic experiences and resiliency study. *Omega: Journal of Death and Dying,* 68(3), 183–205. doi: dx.doi.org/10.2190/OM.68.3.a

Dean, M., McClement, S., Bone, J., Daeninck, P. & Nelson, F. (2005). Parental experiences of adult child death from cancer. *Journal of Palliative Medicine, 8*(4), 751–765.

Dyregrov, K. (2005-2006). Experiences of social networks supporting traumatically bereaved. *Omega: Journal of Death and Dying, 52*(4), 339–358.

Dyregrov, A., Gjestad, R. (2011). Sexuality following the loss of a child. *Death Studies, 35,* 289–315. doi: 10.1080/07481187.2010.527753

Duncan, C. & Cacciatore, J. (2015). A systematic review of the peer-reviewed literature on self-blame, guilt and shame.

Omega: Journal of Death and Dying, 71(4), 312–342. doi: 10.1177/0030222815572604

Elder, J. & Burke, L. (2015). Parental grief expression in online cancer support groups. *Illness, Crisis & Loss, 23*(2), 175–190. doi: 10.1177/1054137315576617

Engelkemeyer, S. & Marwit, S. J. (2008). Posttraumatic growth in bereaved parents. *Journal of Traumatic Stress, 21*(3), June 2008, 344–346. doi: 10.1002/jts.20338

Farnsworth, E. B. & Allen, K. R. (1996). Mothers' bereavement: Experiences of marginalization, stories of change. *Family Relations: An Interdisciplinary Journal of Applied Family Studies, 45*(4), 360–367.

Feigelman, W., Gorman, B., Beal, K. C. & Jordan, J. (2008). Internet support groups for suicide survivors: A new mode for gaining bereavement assistance. *Omega: Journal of Death and Dying, 57*(3), 217–243. doi: 10.2190/OM.57.3.a

Feigelman, W., Jordon, J. & Gorman, B. (2008-2009). How they died, time since loss, and bereavement outcomes. *Omega: Journal of Death and Dying, 58*(4), 251–273. doi: 10.2190/OM.58.4.a

Harper, M., O'Connor, R., Dickson, A. & O'Carroll, R. (2011). Mothers continuing bonds and ambivalence to personal mortality after the death of their child: An interpretative phenomenological analysis. *Psychology, Health & Medicine,* 16(2), 203–214. doi: 10.1080/13548506.2010.532558

Harper, M., O'Connor, R. & O'Carroll, R. (2014). Factors associated with grief and depression following the loss of a child: A multivariate analysis. *Psychology, Health & Medicine,* 19(3), 247–252. doi: 10.1080/13548506.2013.811274

Hunt, S. & Greeff, A. (2011-2012). Parental bereavement: A panoramic view. *Omega: Journal of Death and Dying, 64*(1), 41–63. doi: 10.2190/OM.64.1.d

Klass, D. (1997). The deceased child in the psychic and social worlds of bereaved parents during the resolution of grief. *Death Studies, 21,* 147–175.

Kowalski, S. D. & Bondmass, M. D. (2008). Physiological and psychological symptoms of grief in widows. *Research in Nursing & Health, 31,* 23–30. doi: 10.1002/nur.20228

Kristensen, P., Dyregrov, K., Dyregrov, A. & Heir, T. (2016, March 28). Media exposure and prolonged grief: A study of bereaved parents and siblings after the 2011 Utøya Island terror attack. *Psychological Trauma: Theory, Research, Practice, and Policy.* Advance online publication. http://dx.doi.org/10.1037/tra0000131

Kunkel, A. D. & Dennis, M. R. (2003). Grief consolation in eulogy rhetoric: An integrative framework. *Death Studies, 27,* 1–38. doi: 10.1080/071811

Lehman, D., Ellard, J. & Wortman, C. (1986). Social support for the bereaved: Recipients' and providers' perspectives on what is helpful. *Journal of Counseling and Clinical Psychology*, *54*(4), 438–446.

Lepore, S. H., Silver, R. C., Wortman, C. B. & Wayment, H. A. (1996). Social constraints, intrusive thoughts, and depressive symptoms among bereaved mothers. *Journal of Personality and Social Psychology*, *30*(2), 271–282.

Lichtenthal, W., Currier, J., Neimeyer, R. & Keesee, N. (2010). Sense and significance: A mixed methods examination of meaning making after the loss of one's child. *Journal of Clinical Psychology*, *66*(7),791–812. doi: 10.1002/jclp.20700

Mancini, A., Prati, G. & Black, S. (2011). Self-worth mediates the effects of violent loss on PTSD symptoms. *Journal of Traumatic Stress*, *24*(1), 116–120. doi: 10.1002/jts

McBride, M. C. & Toller, P. (2011). Negotiation of face between bereaved parents and their social networks. *Southern Communication Journal*, *76*(3), 210–229. doi: 10.1080/10417940903477647

Miers, D., Abbott, D. & Springer, P. (2012). A phenomenological study of family needs following the suicide of a teenager. *Death Studies*, *36*, 118–133. doi: 10.1080/07481187.2011.553341

Miles, M. S. (1985). Emotional symptoms and physical health in bereaved parents. *Nursing Research, 34*(2), 76–81.

Murphy, S., Braun, T., Tillery, L., Cain, K. C., Johnson, L. C. & Beaton, R. D. (1999). PTSD among bereaved parents following the violent deaths of their 12- to 28-year-old children: A longitudinal prospective analysis. *Journal of Traumatic Stress, 12*(2), 273–291.

Murphy, S., Johnson, L. & Lohan, J. (2002). The aftermath of the violent death of a child: An integration of the assessments of parents' mental distress and PTSD during the first 5 years of bereavement. *Journal of Loss and Trauma, 7,* 203–222. doi: 10.1080=10811440290057620

Murphy, S., Johnson, L. & Lohan, J. (2003). The effectiveness of coping resources and strategies used by bereaved parents 1 and 5 years after the violent deaths of their children. *Omega: Journal of Death and Dying, 47,* 25–44.

Nikkola, I., Kaunonen, M. & Aho, A. L. (2013). Mother's experience of the support from a bereavement follow-up intervention after the death of a child. *Journal of Clinical Nursing, 22,* 1151–1162. doi: 10.1111/j.1365-2702.2012.04247.x

Norton, M. & Francesca, G. (2014). Rituals alleviate grieving for loved ones, lovers and lotteries. *Journal of Experimental Psychology: General,* 143(1), 266–272. doi: 10.1037/a0031772

Oliver, R., Sturlevant, J., Scheetz, J. & Fallat, M. E. (2001). Beneficial effects of a hospital bereavement intervention program after traumatic childhood death. *The Journal of Trauma, Injury, Infection, and Critical Care, 50,* 440–448.

Pope, C. (March, 2007). From the chapter leader. *The Compassionate Friends: North Shore—Boston Chapter Newsletter.*

Rack, J. J., Burleson, B. R., Bodie, G. D., Holmstrom, A. J. & Servaty-Seib, H. (2008). Bereaved adults' evaluations of grief management: Effects of message person centeredness, recipient individual differences, and contextual factors. *Death Studies,* 32, 399–427. doi. 10.1080/07481180802006711

Riches, G. & Dawson, P. (1998). Lost children, living memories: The role of photographs in processes of grief adjustment among bereaved parents. *Death Studies, 22*(2), 121–140.

Rogers, C., Floyd, F., Seltzer, M., Greenberg, J. & Hong, J. (2008). Long-term effects of the death of a child on parents' adjustment in midlife. *Journal of Family Psychology, 22*(2), 203–211. doi: 10.1037/0893-3200.22.2.203

Rossetto, K. (2014). Creating philanthropic foundations to deal with grief: Case studies of bereaved parents. *Death Studies, 38,* 531–537. doi: 10.1080/07481187.2014.899652

Schwab, R. (1996). Bereaved parents and support group participation. *Omega: Journal of Death and Dying, 32*(1), 49–61.

Sin, N. L. & Lyubomirsky, S. (2009). Enhancing well-being and alleviating depressive symptoms with positive psychology interventions: A practice-friendly meta-analysis. *Journal of Clinical Psychology: In Session, 65*(5), 467–487. doi: 10.1002/jclp.20593

Somanti, M. & August, J. (1997). Parental bereavement: Spiritual connections with deceased children. *American Journal of Orthopsychiatry, 67,* 460–469.

Spratt, M. L. & Denny, D. R. (1991). Immune variables, depression, and plasma cortisol over time in suddenly bereaved parents. *The Journal of Neuropsychiatry and Clinical Neurosciences, 3*(3), 299–306.

Sittser, J. (2004). *A grace disguised: How the soul grows through loss.* Grand Rapids, MI: Zondervan.

Stroebe, M., Finkenauer, C., Wijngaards-de Meij, L., Schut, H., Van den Bout, J. & Stroebe, W. (2013). Partner-oriented self-regulation among bereaved parents: The costs of holding in grief for the partner's sake. *Psychological Science, 24*(4), 395–402. doi:10.1177/0956797612457383

Stroebe, M., Schut, H. & Stroebe, W. (2007). Health outcomes in bereavement. *Lancet, 370,* 1960–73.

Sundell, S. E. (1998). An investigation of parental bereavement: Health-promoting factors in bereavement outcome[s]. *Dissertation Abstracts, 58*(12A), 4572.

Talbot, K. (1997). Mothers now childless: Survival after the death of an only child. *Omega: Journal of Death and Dying, 34*(3), 177–189.

Tan, J., Docherty, S., Barfield, R. & Brandon, D. (2012). Addressing parental bereavement support needs at the end of life for infants with complex chronic conditions. *Journal of Palliative Medicine, 15*(5), 579–584. doi: 10.1089/jpm.2011.0357

Thompson, A., Miller, K., Barrera, M., Davies, B., Foster, T., Gilmer, M. J.,...Gerhardt, C. (2011). A qualitative study of advice from bereaved parents and siblings. *Journal of Social Work in End-of-Life & Palliative Care, 7*, 153–172. doi: 10.1080/15524256.2011.593153

Thrift, O. & Coyle, A. (2005). An interpretative phenomenological analysis of maternal identity following child suicide: Abridged. *Counseling Psychology Review, 20*(2), 18–23.

Thuen, F. (1997). Received social support from informal networks and professionals in bereavement. *Psychology, Health & Medicine, 2*(1), 51–63. doi: 10.1080/13548599708400560

Titus, B. & de Souza, R. (2011). Finding meaning in the loss of a child: Journeys of chaos and quest. *Health Communication, 26*(5a), 450–460. doi: 10.1080/10410236.2011.554167

Toblin, R. L., Riviere, L. A., Thomas, J. L., Adler, A. B., Kok, B. C. & Hoge, C. W. (2012). Grief and physical health outcomes in US soldiers returning from combat. *Journal of AffectiveDisorders, 136,*469–475.doi:10.1016/j.jad.2011.10.048

Toller, P. W. (2005). Negotiation of dialectical contradictions by parents who have experienced the death of a child. *Journal of Applied Communication Research, 33*(1), 46–66. doi: 10.1080/00909880042000318512

Utz, R., Caserta, M. & Lund, D. (2011). Grief, depressive symptoms, and physical health among recently bereaved spouses. *The Gerontologist, 52*(4), 460–471. doi:10.1093/geront/gnr110

Wijngaards-de Meij, L., Stroebe, M., Stroebe, W., Schut, H., Van den Bout, J., Van der Heijden, P. & Dijkstra, I. (2008). The impact of circumstances surrounding the death of a child on parents' grief. *Death Studies, 32,* 237–252. doi: 10.1080/07481180701881263

Wijngaards-de Meij, L., Stroebe, M., Schut, H., Stroebe, W., Van den Bout, J., Van der Heijden, P. & Dijkstra, I. (2005). Couples at risk following the death of their child: Predictors of grief versus depression. *Journal of Consulting and Clinical Psychology, 73*(4), 617–623. doi: 10.1037/0022-006X.73.4.617

Wing, D., Clance, P. R., Burge-Callaway, K. & Armistead, L. (2001). Understanding gender differences in bereavement following the death of an infant: Implications for treatment. *Psychotherapy: Theory, Research, Practice, Training, 3*(1), 60–73.

Woodgate, R. (2006). Living in a world without closure: Reality for parents who have experienced the death of a child. *Journal of Palliative Care, 22*(2), 75–82.

Made in the USA
Coppell, TX
03 February 2020

15339829R00095